THE LAND OF MOONLIT SNOWS

An engineer from the University of California, Berkeley, and a trekker by choice, Gaurav Punj has been exploring the Indian Himalaya since 2006. Through his books and his venture, Connect with Himalaya, he aims to do his bit to spotlight the lesser known Himalaya and demystify trekking as an activity everyone can enjoy.

THE LAND OF MOONLIT SNOWS

& OTHER REAL TRAVEL STORIES FROM THE INDIAN HIMALAYA

GAURAV PUNJ

First published by Tranquebar, an imprint of Westland Publications Private Limited, in 2018

Published by Tranquebar, an imprint of Westland Books, a division of Nasadiya Technologies Private Limited, in 2024

No. 269/2B, First Floor, 'Irai Arul', Vimalraj Street, Nethaji Nagar, Alapakkam Main Road, Maduravoyal, Chennai 600095

Westland, the Westland logo, Tranquebar and the Tranquebar logo are the trademarks of Nasadiya Technologies Private Limited, or its affiliates.

ISBN: 9789357768405

10 9 8 7 6 5 4 3 2 1

Typeset by SŪRYA, New Delhi

Printed at Saurabh Printers Pvt. Ltd

To the shepherds of Himalaya,
on whose trails all trekkers tread

CONTENTS

FOREWORD

Trekking is a means to an end; and the end of a Himalayan trek is to release something real within us. In a disjointed world, trekking helps gladden the heart or, if you prefer it, put a shine on the soul. As going on a trek usually connotes an arduous hike over challenging terrain, the services of a guide is a wise investment to save time, not to mention one's neck. Everyone's life is a road to self-discovery and when we come to unmarked crossroads, a good guide makes all the difference.

Gaurav's books are meant for the busy, intelligent, time-bound urban reader and provide creative insights in innovative formats. Crucially, he understands the need to liaise with the local people to harness their expertise so both parties benefit from the harmonious relationship. Connecting with the Himalayan village stakeholders is something colonial mountaineers, for obvious reasons—with the exception of climbers like Frank Smythe and Eric Shipton—avoided.

The extraordinary diversity of the Himalayan terrain means that every trekker can expect to find their level of plenitude, or even better, respond to the extremes on offer. The contrast between the familiar alpine greenery of the southern aspect and the stark, treeless landscape of Ladakh immediately after you cross the Zoji La astounds, as does the less obvious difference between the gentle rise of the southern slopes, leading to a dramatic near-perpendicular drop in places, to declare the northern face.

The book's nine stories cover the field from Sikkim to Ladakh and present personal reminiscences that linger for the unique character and identity of the area visited. Rujuta also brings alive the beauty of the rolling landscape at Dayara, with the added excitement of a nocturnal prowler of the hair-raising variety. While most trekkers avoid the monsoon drench, it is in fact the only time you can experience the full Monty of the Himalayan display of erotic floral wilfulness. Nature at a higher altitude has a short span to flower in fragrant abandon to attract the birds and the bees, and only in her blessed meadows in the rains does she pull out all the stops. Gaurav and his friends' dicey, hence unforgettable encounter with the slopes above Manali, proves how in the misty mid-region can be found all the challenges you can hope for, capped by the promise of a hot shower only hours away.

As a fragile ecology, the Himalayan ecosystem needs careful monitoring. The 'Abode of Snow' risks becoming a misnomer and the flow of Himalayan rivers have reduced to mere dribbles. Climate change can be witnessed daily: recently, I spotted on my Mussoorie walk, a lantana bush (normally found at low altitudes) flowering in February, alongside a much higher species in bloom, the rhododendron. Another change is the gradual disappearance of the nomadic shepherd who, at high altitudes, proves to be a trekker's best friend in sticky situations, and a most hospitable companion. Thanks to the cell phone and its consumer blandishments, there are few recruits for the exposed and exacting job of counting sheep these days.

At the start of even the most modest trek, the advice of the Matterhorn survivor, Edward Whymper, should be taken seriously: 'Think at the beginning what the end may be.' Make sure your outing ends with a bang and not with a Whymper, and raise a toast to that intoxicating William James formula, which a Himalayan trek can be trusted to deliver—'From the chill periphery to the radiant core.'

Bill Aitken
June 2018
Mussoorie

A SHORT NOTE FOR READERS

Hi. Thank you for buying the book. And even before that, a big thanks to everyone who bought and read *The Land of Flying Lamas*, and gave me the reason and the chance to write *The Land of Moonlit Snows*. Conventional wisdom says that the second book is always the toughest to write. My publishers surely must subscribe to that thought, considering the amount of leeway they gave me to finish this book. But to be honest, it wasn't. Most of the time I took was in procrastinating, true to the spirit of the laid-back places I travel to and write about. Places where the city folk look at their watches and say things like, 'It's 8 a.m. here, must be noon in Mumbai.' Only when time stands still, do we acknowledge it, feel it. And that, ladies and gentlemen, is reason 101 that you must go to the mountains.

In this book, just like in my first, I tell stories from my trips, stories which invariably manifest themselves when city people meet the mountains. When tears and fears go along with laughter and triumph. The stories take place in the 'other' Himalaya I introduced in *The Land of Flying Lamas*. The 90 per cent where less than 10 per cent tourists go. Not much has changed in the last four years. We still see the same pattern—a trek becomes popular on FB / Insta and everyone wants to go there to take the same pictures they saw online, from the same angle. The latest entrants to this dubious list of trips are the Chaddar trek in Zanskar and the Spiti road journey.

Both these are extremely fragile ecosystems but make for excellent profile pictures, so who cares. But here is the thing. If one can go to a place, why can't the other? Why judge harshly? And that's a perfectly fine argument. You don't have to not go to places you want to go just because they are popular, but there are some basic rules you can follow to minimise the impact of your visit.

Rules for sustainable tourism

1. Travel in small groups, ideally twelve or less.
2. As much as possible, get in touch directly with local guides, porters, cooks, drivers, etc., in the region that you are going to visit and plan your trip with them. There are small, local trekking organisations almost everywhere you can trek.
3. Minimise the packaged foods you bring and eat local, freshly-cooked food as often as possible. Yes, on treks too.
4. Choose local family-run guesthouses over hotels and homestays over guesthouses.
5. Don't litter. Make sure you leave nothing behind on the trail or campsite.
6. Don't play loud music when staying in villages or on campsites.

Of course, the golden rule still is—spread out. There are just too many places to explore.

Coming back to the stories in this book. The toughest decision as always was—which stories to tell. For the last ten years, I have been leading roughly twelve group trips every year (Connect with Himalaya), so there was a decent enough base to choose from. Three or four stories selected themselves, because something really exciting, funny or scary happened during those trips. But it's not in every trip that you get stranded in remote valleys, or get lost in snowstorms. Most of the time, the stories are made of small things—sights, conversations, meals, etc.—which accumulate during the course of the trip, instead of one incident or one thrilling day, and it's the setting which is the true hero. Most of the stories in the book are these accumulated experiences of people like you and me on travels to some really remote, untouched places in the Indian Himalaya.

Before every story, I have mentioned a bit about the place to provide a context. The details I have kept for the end, under the 'Guide' section—detailed day-by-day itineraries (twenty-five in total) covering almost the entire Indian Himalaya, along with some local contacts. I feel that this is the easiest and most straightforward way for you to actually go to the places you will read about, and for me to give you actionable information. I do hope the stories inspire you to travel to the Himalaya, to explore new places, to meet local people, live with them, eat with them, share experiences with them. If it does, the book would be worth the paper it is printed on.

Gaurav Punj
June 2018
Mumbai

Hand-drawn maps for representation purposes only.
Not to scale.

LADAKH

The adventures of a boy who forgot

It was 2009. The roads in Ladakh were still very much like they were everywhere else in the mountains, which means, practically non-existent. They gave the whole hour-by-hour planning, the number of stops to be taken, where to have lunch and tea, etc., an urgency, a meaning. Not that I rue the smooth roads in Ladakh today, but it's just not the same. The only thing that remains a constant is the absolutely mind-blowing landscape which never ceases to amaze. Like I always do for all my Ladakh trips, we started from Srinagar and followed the centuries-old Silk Route, with stopovers at Sonmarg, Kargil and Alchi before we reached Leh. On the way, we crossed the Greater Himalayan range at Zoji La and the Zanskar range at Namik La and Fotu La, which besides adding to the adventure, gave us an understanding of the gradual change in landscape, the people, their food and their culture.

Once in Leh, we rested for a couple of days, before making the usual trips to Nubra Valley and Pangong Lake. These two outings were interspersed by a short trek to Rumbak village and a homestay there, when we had a chance to actually get to know the gentle, kind and big-hearted Ladakhis, the type who not just survive, but thrive in one of the most inhospitable terrains in the world. The trip was full of stories, as all trips to Ladakh usually are, but this is the story of a boy, a member of our group, who was so forgetful that he forgot even that.

Gautam is the most forgetful person I have ever met. Within the first two days of the trip starting from Srinagar, he had trained all of us to look after him. Not by invoking our love and care, but just our instinct for self-preservation. I mean, no one likes to wait or drive back to pick up forgotten sunglasses, a camera case, sweater … or one of the million things that he invariably forgot at every place we stopped on the way. It was easier to just quickly scan the surroundings once he got up after having his cup of tea or momos, and pick up after him. Those were the early days of Ladakh's new-found status as a must-go destination. The roads were broken, petrol pumps few and far in between, and drivers had a laid-back attitude. Basically, what you would expect from a remote, high Himalayan place which is not yet a Facebook must-go.

From Srinagar to Sonmarg on the first day, to Kargil on Day 2, and finally to Leh on Day 3, the daily driving hours increased exponentially, so did the thrill of the ride and the excitement of reaching Leh, in the heart of Ladakh. Our group was faring well, with frequent food stops and regular water intake. The gradual gain of altitude ensured that we avoided most of the perceived horrors of the journey to the top of the world. The dreaded words, 'altitude sickness', stayed out of our daily discussion and around 6 p.m. on the third day of being on the road, we reached Leh (check the picture on page i of the inserts). Always a momentous moment for me, then and every time since then.

After thoroughly checking all the cars for any of Gautam's belongings, we checked into our guesthouse in the Changspa area of Leh. We had a quick briefing which went like this—'Hope all of you are feeling well. We can now just chill and relax and if you want, you can go out for a short walk in the Leh bazaar. But if you are feeling even a hint of discomfort, just rest and you will be fine by tomorrow morning.'

When everyone had dispersed to put their luggage in their rooms, Gautam told me that he was going to rest as he was feeling a bit tired. The rest of us got together after a while and went for a stroll outside. The Leh market was a much nicer place then, no traffic jams, no incessant honking, and no fear of actually being run over by tourist bikes or cars. We had a good time sipping ginger lemon honey at a coffee shop and shortlisting shops to visit later in the trip. When we returned to the guesthouse after a couple of hours, we were met by a hassled-looking Sonam, the guesthouse owner, at the gate.

'Sir, the ambulance will be reaching anytime.'

'What?' I asked loudly.

'Your friend, he is not feeling well and has called for an ambulance.'

I rushed into Gautam's room and this was the scene that greeted me: dark room, curtains drawn, lights off, a figure sitting up on the bed.

'What happened?' I asked, as I switched on the lights.

'Nothing yaar, just a headache. So I called my friends back home and they told me to go to a hospital and get some oxygen.'

'Have you had enough water today?'

'I forgot.'

I poured him a glass of water and patiently explained to him, once again, that he didn't need oxygen. That it was okay, and he just needed to hydrate, eat a bit and rest it out. By tomorrow morning, he would be totally fine.

'Yes, I know. But oxygen won't harm, na?'

'No, it won't. But neither will it help. You will unnecessarily go to hospital.'

By that time, everyone else in the group had gathered in his room. The consensus amongst them was that if he wanted to, I should let him go to hospital. And on cue,

Sonam came in with the news that the ambulance had arrived. A couple of guys offered to accompany us and we were soon on our way to the hospital.

The hospital in Leh is run by the Army and is just outside the airport, merely a ten-minute drive from Changspa. At the reception, we were asked for a two-rupee fee, in exact change. We didn't have any, and since she refused to accept any other denomination, we had to borrow a coin from the ambulance driver. We were then asked to meet Dr Dorje in her consultation room. She was a young doctor, but had clearly dealt with enough of such 'need oxygen' episodes.

'Who is the patient?'

Gautam raised his hand sheepishly.

'What happened?'

'Altitude sickness.'

'Diagnose toh kar hi liya, now tell me what you need as well.'

'Oxygen.'

'Okay, it won't help much but I am writing you a ten-minute dose. Where are you guys from?'

'Mumbai,' we chorused.

'Hmm, how come you are missing the Ganesh festival?'

Gulrayz replied as if he had prepared for this question, 'Ma'am, Gautam has come to look for a girl here, to get hitched.'

'Won't work. He will get altitude sickness here and she will get sea sick in Mumbai.'

We giggled like school kids, and realising that she was far too smart for us, took Gautam to the oxygen room.

The sight of him lying on the bed, mask on his face, surrounded by all of us and the laughing nurses, was well worth the visit.

Actually, just meeting Dr Dorje was.

The trek to Rumbak

After acclimatising in Leh for a couple of days, we went to the Nubra Valley across the Khardung La Pass, saw the hidden lake at Panamic, stayed the night in cottages in a nice organic garden, and on the way back to Leh, had a (world's highest) snow fight just below Khardung La.

Next on our agenda was the trek to the village of Rumbak, a day's walk from the nearest roadhead. We were to stay in the village, in homestays with local people, and use that time to talk to them, eat with them and in general, try and understand their way of life. Homestays, done right, remain the best windows to the lives of locals in the Himalaya. We had a quick briefing in the night—it's easy enough, everyone can do it without any trouble since the height gain is very gradual, etc. I also told everyone to carry only a small backpack, with one change of clothes, woollens, sunscreen, hat, sunglasses and a water bottle.

In the morning, we drove to the small settlement of Zingchen, the roadhead and the starting point of the trek. There we met Tundup, our guide, and he gave each of us a box with some snacks, which was to be our lunch on the way. He had also hired a pack mule, in case we didn't want to carry our small backpacks, and promptly, quite a few unburdened themselves.

It was an enjoyable walk, the trail passing through a narrow valley first and then reaching the open grounds just outside Rumbak village. The trail continues on to Stok La, a pass at almost 4,900 metres, which is amongst the most popular treks in Ladakh. Rumbak lies just before the big climb to the pass. It is part of the Hemis National Park and is also the hub of all the expeditions to see the snow leopard in winter.

We were a happy bunch when we reached the village in the afternoon after our easy walk, relieved that the daunting climb to the pass was not part of our itinerary. Tundup took us to one of the bigger homes, where we all settled in the kitchen. He then went out to organise the other homestays. It works on rotation and every household that has enrolled gets its turn to host visitors. A very fair and practical system. Check the picture on page i of the inserts, of Rumbak and its homes.

LEAVE THE CHADDAR ALONE

Come winter, many rivers and lakes freeze in the high Himalaya. A natural phenomenon. But not all frozen rivers have a significance. The Zanskar River in Ladakh does. When it freezes over in winter, it becomes the only route to reach Leh for the Zanskaris, who are otherwise cut off from all civilisation. But it's not an adventure for them, it's a need. They understand the perils of walking on a frozen river, in a deep gorge. They pray to the spirits of the Zanskar to let them cross safely. The river is sacred for them.

Since 2011, when it was featured in a BBC documentary and subsequently termed 'the wildest trek in the world', there has been a hundred-fold increase in the number of people attempting the Chaddar trek. Where just about 100 Zanskaris would walk over the river in the roughly two months it is frozen, more than 7,000 trekkers went for the trek in 2016, camping in overcrowded, filthy sites along the river.

One river. A hundred-plus trekkers a day. How much bio waste would be generated daily? Where does it go? The sacred Zanskar. The river which is the lifeline of the locals. What about the heat generated? How much has it raised the average temperature of the area? Its effect on the river? If the river does not freeze, for visitors, it just means not completing the trek. However, for locals, it means taking the far riskier route along the sides of the steep gorge.

And then, the trekking ethics. Do the trekkers who opt for Chaddar understand the geography, the ecology and the culture of this place? Do they understand the ethos of trekking without leaving a trace? Have they trekked before in the Himalaya? Have they understood the gradual changes in terrain, in the weather, in the entire way of life, as one moves from the lower hills to the meadows and streams of the middle Himalaya; and then to the passes across the Greater Himalaya connecting to the trans-Himalaya? Have they just flown over the whole expanse of the Himalaya to land straight in Ladakh, and then fallen into a long line of other trekkers with their bags hauled by porters? Do they really believe that this is the wildest trek in the world?

The Chaddar trek has, unfortunately, become a marker of how much you don't care for the ecology of the Himalaya, the ethics of trekking and the culture and rights of the local people. It's the 'Facebook trek' of this decade.

The Himalaya has a lot to offer. Don't be greedy. Spread out.

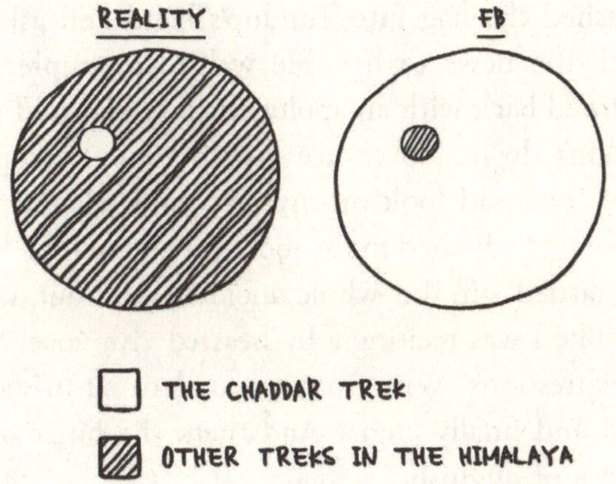

• • •

While we were talking about this and admiring the utensils and crockery on display along the four walls of the kitchen, Tundup came in looking hassled and asked me if I could step out.

'Sir, the mule went a little crazy. It threw away a few bags and even stomped on one. Everything is okay now, but one bag has got damaged.'

I had seen this happen before, so I was not too bothered, till he showed me the bag. For one, it was in tatters. Second, and more importantly, it belonged to Sirisha, the fashionista of the group. Inside were a pair of jeans and a jacket, coated with a thick paste of what we later figured out was mud + eggs + sandwich + boiled potato + juice + chocolate—the contents of our lunch boxes.

I pushed the bag into Tundup's hand and asked him to break the news to her. He walked a couple of feet, then turned back with an apologetic face and told me that he couldn't do it. No choice now but to chin up, sport a serious plus sad look on my face, and tell the truth.

My bravery ditched me as soon as I entered the kitchen. And I rattled off the whole incident without taking a breath, like I was reciting a by-hearted viva voce. Sirisha's facial expressions went from amused to surprised, then shocked and finally angry. And then, she burst out into loud cries of anguish.

'This was my favourite jacket, my aunt got it from London. I hate you, Kanu. I hate Ladakh, and hate you the most, GP!'

With some choice gaalis for her friends and me, she finally collapsed in Kanu's lap.

Everyone went deathly quiet. Even the homestay host stopped midway in her momo preparation. The only sounds in the room were Sirisha's sobs. Tundup, the gentle, couldn't take it anymore. He picked up the battered jeans and jacket, and declared thus: 'I promise, Sirisha madam, I will wash your clothes first thing in the morning and by the time we leave from this village, they will be as good as new.'

The inconsolable Sirisha couldn't bear to look at her clothes and just waved him away with a 'le jao sab'. One by one, all of us tip-toed out of the house and after we reached a safe distance, burst into laughter like the cheapsters we all are, inherently.

As it so happened, the next morning, we woke up to snowfall and it didn't stop till it was time to leave. Tundup never really got the chance to wash Sirisha's clothes. We had to wrap them in a cheap plastic bag and hand them over to her. Even though she got them washed and cleaned in Leh, Sirisha would often sniff at her jacket, shake her head and exclaim, 'It still smells of egg, man!'

The secret pact

Other than the episode with Sirisha, things went as per plan. Everyone had a great time in their respective homestays. When we met in the evening, there was an actual argument over whose homestay food was the best, with all of us identifying ourselves with our host families and fighting to uphold their culinary superiority. Tundup, who was still his resolute self, informed us that there was a village get- together that night after dinner, and that we were all invited. Village get-togethers in the Himalaya invariably mean song and dance, and this was exactly what happened.

Almost the entire village was packed in the community hall by 8 p.m. The slow, but rhythmic Ladakhi dance started almost immediately. Very soon, chang (a drink made from barley, brewed at home) was being passed around. It was compulsory for the guests to have it, we were told. And then everyone, men and women, were dancing and singing with gay abandon, without missing a step or a beat.

After a couple of hours, my trip leader persona kicked in and I asked Tundup how long this was going to go on.

'Till everyone leaves with their partner for the night,' he replied.

When I told the group that it was time to go, no one resisted as all of us were dead tired. A warm blanket, a hot water bag and the insulated stone and mud homes soon lulled us into deep sleep on that cold night.

But there was more to the quiet night. Unbeknownst to me, a secret pact had been forged and a plan was afoot. This had happened back in Leh, after my talk about the trek where I had also mentioned the homestays and the dry-pit toilets, and how they were very eco-friendly, zero waste and clean, etc. Four members of our group got together in one of their rooms and, in hushed voices, thrashed out this plan: we don't believe this 'dry-toilet being clean and odourless' speech, and we hereby commit to not using the toilet at all throughout our stay in that village, we cross our hearts. After a couple of minutes of silence during which they must have visualised how it would be not to use the toilet at all, the plan was modified as follows: we will not use the toilet for the big job, only to pee.

So while most of us were sleeping soundly, the fantastic four took out deos from their bags, covered their faces with mufflers and tip-toed to their respective dry-pit toilets under the starry night at 4,000 metres. They first 'deodorised' the toilet by spraying tonnes of deo, then made a quick dash in, all the while holding their breaths, and then rushed out. With the deed done, they quietly slipped back into their rooms, and went to bed feeling quite thrilled with the whole thing.

How did I get to know all this? Just read till the end. It's worth it.

We woke up the next morning to a white Rumbak. Fluffy snow was still falling, and even though it was bitterly cold, we just had to be out. After a couple of failed attempts at a replay of the snow fight, we rushed back in as our hands had frozen. We sat around the kitchen fire along with our sensible hosts, and once we were warm, enjoyed the snowfall from the small kitchen window. We ate Ladakhi bread with yak cheese, drank butter tea churned in a long vessel and chatted for what felt like eternity. The snowfall stopped and the sun peeped out from behind the clouds. Tundup stuck his head into the kitchen and announced that it was time to leave. He then dashed off to the next homestay to make the same announcement. Quick goodbyes, some pictures with the hosts, a rendezvous at the village entrance under the yak heads and soon we were back on the trail. It was just 9 a.m., Himalaya standard time.

And he forgets

We walked in quiet admiration of the surreal landscape and the tremendous scale of the Himalaya, putting our lives in perspective. I don't know how, or if meditation works or what it even means really … but if it's about connecting to your thoughts, there is nothing better you can do than to walk the Himalayan trails. And it's always on the way back, when you know what lies ahead, that you truly relax and appreciate the mountains.

My reverie was broken by the sight of Gautam rushing towards me from in front of the group. And maybe because of my meditative state, or just plain experience, I knew that he had forgotten something.

'My … wallet,' he said, panting, and pointing towards Rumbak. We had walked for about thirty minutes. I told him to go back with Tundup and look for it, while I waited there for him. The horseman was to continue with the rest of the group.

They returned after an hour and a half and even from a distance, I could see it had been a futile search. Gautam was walking with drooped shoulders, and as he approached me, he shook his head to indicate that he hadn't found it.

'We looked everywhere, yaar. My credit and debit cards, driving licence, PAN card, car RC, everything gone. I don't even have an id to catch my flight back home. I know it's my fault only, but it sucks. I need to get to Leh and make calls to cancel all the cards.'

Tundup, the gentle, was looking more gutted than Gautam was, and had put a hand on Gautam's shoulder. I said something on the lines of: 'I am sorry, but it happens, we will be in Leh shortly and you can get an id faxed from home.'

Realising that we couldn't do anything about it, we started walking again. We caught up with the rest of the group towards the end of the trail. Most were sympathetic towards Gautam, some gently admonished him and a few had a 'we knew it was coming' expression. By 3 p.m., we were in the guesthouse and everyone split to do their own thing. The BIG day was up next.

THINGS TO DO IN LEH

- Chill in the coffee shops or the bakeries and roadside stalls which are always buzzing with activity and getting better each year. There are also bookshops and shops which sell ethically-sourced local produce.
- If you want to do something more 'active', you can hire a mountain bike or a motorbike to ride in and around Leh. There is also the option of going rafting on the Indus or the Zanskar. If you have done rafting in Rishikesh, you will find the rapids here very ordinary, but the landscape is spectacular.
- One of the important aspects of acclimatising here, is eating good food. You can choose anything from Tibetan cuisine to pizzas to Continental ... to almost every possible kind of food you know. New restaurants open each year, so it's best that you check before you leave for Leh, either with friends who have been there recently or online, on rating websites.

- Now that Leh is a bonafide hill station rivalling Shimla, Manali, etc., there is no dearth of 'points'. Shanti Stupa, Thicksey Monastery, Shey Palace, War Museum continue to be the most popular ones.
- Strolling in the pedestrian-only Leh market seems to be the favourite pastime for everyone these days, so you should check it out once at least.

• • •

A visit to Pangong

Pangong Tso is a magical place. Geographically, it has very few parallels in the world—a salt water lake at 4,200 metres, 120 km long, 10 km wide, divided between India and Tibet (now China). Just the journey to get to Pangong should put it on the 'things to do before you die' list. This was 2009. *3 Idiots* was yet to release and unfairly take the blame for what is essentially a civic issue—the crowds littering the exact place they have travelled for days to see.

Coming back to our story. Relatively fewer people went to Pangong then, and that was because it was a long and tough day's journey from Leh to the lake and back. But that was what made it such a big thing. We discussed the long journey, how to manage time, food and water, etc., in our nightly talk, and decided that 5.30 a.m. was when we would leave. If all went well, we would be back by 6 p.m. Everyone was super excited about Pangong and even followed my advice of going to bed early.

When everyone had gone to bed, Gautam came up to me. He was still down because of the loss of his wallet, but he was also looking a bit sick.

'I am not feeling good, I am gonna rest tomorrow. You guys have fun.'

'Oh, are you sure? You know we have kept the best for the last.'

But he insisted that he wanted to stay back. And with that, we turned in.

The next morning, everything went like clockwork. We were on the road by 5.45 a.m., having had a quick breakfast of bread toast and fruits. Our water bottles and camera batteries were full. It was a gorgeous day. One that makes everything sparkle and keeps you in wonderment throughout. The road, the mountains, the Chang La Pass and the Changthang plateau, were mesmerising. We even spotted some shy marmots (not so shy these days as visitors have started feeding them chips) and kiang (the Tibetan wild ass) on the wide, flat, grassy land, that is characteristic of Changthang. We crossed a pagal nullah (streams that cascade down strongly from the mountainside, changing their line of flow every year, wreaking havoc on the road—therefore termed 'pagal nullah' or 'mad streams' in the Himalaya), turned a bend and spotted a blue ribbon floating in the distance, the waters of Pangong, the first sight. Till date, this first view of Pangong still manages to take my breath away like nothing else ever does. And then we were on the shores of the great lake.

After the initial few minutes of screaming and shouting and clamouring for pictures (selfies were not a thing yet, can you believe that), all of us felt like being on our own. We drifted away from each other, sitting or lying down by the shore, in our own slice of heaven, in our own thoughts. You will know what I mean when you are there. Take a look at this picture till then on page i of the inserts.

Speeding up things now. We realised that no amount of time was going to be enough and said our goodbyes. Paid a quick visit to the Army souvenir shop, had something to eat at a makeshift dhaba and were soon on our way back. A perfect drive later, we reached Leh and were greeted by the sight of Sonam, once again, at the gate. Déjà vu.

'Sir, your friend has been hospitalised.'

We turned the cars around, got to the hospital in ten minutes, found out where Gautam was and rushed to the room. A dejected Gautam was sitting propped up against the wall on a hospital bed. As soon as he saw us, a sheepish smile appeared on his face.

'I am not here for oxygen.'

'What happened?' we all shouted.

'Piles.'

There was stunned silence.

'Piles?'

'What does that even mean?'

'How the hell did you get piles?'

'I forgot I have a history of piles.'

And then he looked at Sirisha, Kanu and Moksh, and spilled the beans—the secret pact, holding on and not doing the big job in Rumbak, and so on. Wow. It was so ludicrous; we didn't know how to react. But we chose the laughter route and were soon backslapping each other and the fab four.

'The lady doctor is saying I can't go home for three days. I want to go home, please help,' Gautam was appealing to our better nature. We ignored him for another five minutes.

Anyway, after many requests and assurances from us on Gautam's behalf, the doctor agreed to give him an injection which would keep things under control for five hours, after which 'anything can happen, don't blame me later'. We booked him on the next morning's flight and the entire group turned up to take him to the airport. Sitting in a wheelchair, injected with whatever that puts a lid on it for five hours, without his wallet but with his sense of humour and the goofy smile intact, he waved us goodbye at the entrance. This was to be our last day in Leh, kept solely for shopping and chilling. We spent most of it talking about the Rumbak episode over plates of momos at the Tibetan Kitchen.

P.S.: The Gautam saga was not over yet. In the afternoon, when I returned to the guesthouse, Tundup was waiting for me. He wanted me to come with him to the trekking team's office, as something important had come up. At the office, I was handed a package, rolled inside which was Gautam's wallet, with everything intact. The people at the homestay he was staying in couldn't get over the fact that their guest had lost something while in Rumbak. They kept looking for it and finally found it in the dry-pit toilet of the adjacent homestay where Gautam's friends of the secret pact had stayed. He had used their toilet the one time he had needed to pee, and had forgotten about it. That's one place he had not searched.

Tashi, the young girl from the homestay, had walked to Leh, deposited the wallet and walked back to Rumbak.

'Why you didn't ask her to stay back, we would have thanked her,' I asked Tundup.

'She was happy they had found the wallet. Walking here and back is not a big deal, but to have something missing in their village is.'

THE GUIDE

To truly soak in Ladakh, you have to give yourself time. Time and a proper itinerary which will allow you to appreciate the changing terrain as you go from the green side of the Himalaya to the stark brown, and help you acclimatise on the way. Although almost everyone follows the standard Ladakh itinerary now, there is still scope to make small alterations which will take you to less-visited places and allow you a better chance to get to know Ladakh the way it was before the flood gates of tourism opened.

ITINERARY 1:
THE LADAKH INITIATION

Category: Road trip.

Recommended for: Your first trip to Ladakh.

Who can do this: Everyone, age and fitness levels no bar.

How long: 9 days.

When: May to October.

- Day 1: Reach Srinagar. Either fly in or get there by road. You can choose to stay the night in Srinagar or drive for couple of hours to Sonmarg and spend the night there.
- Day 2: Drive to Kargil via Zoji La and Drass. The first big change in landscape happens today. Kargil is as old and important a town as Leh is, from the silk trade times.
- Day 3: Drive to Alchi. It's only one-and-a-half hours from Leh, but a day here gives you an idea of how Leh was ten years ago—laid-back and cool.
- Day 4: Reach Leh. Take it easy today, just walk around the market and chill.
- Day 5: Explore Leh. More chilling, and if you are up for it, some mountain biking or riding or rafting or sightseeing.
- Day 6: Drive to Nubra Valley via Khardung La. Visit the hidden lake at Panamic and the sand

dunes at Hunder. Stay the night in one of many fancy places there.

- Day 7: Drive to Pangong along the Shyok River. If you had come to Ladakh twenty years ago, all roads were like this. Stunning and with no one around for miles. The road is seasonal, so find out beforehand if it's open. Else, take the Wari La route to Pangong. Once in Pangong, choose a camp which is away from the lake so that you minimise your contribution towards destroying the lake.
- Day 8: Drive back to Leh. Finish any shopping that's left.
- Day 9: Fly out of Leh.

ITINERARY 1A (if you have four extra days)

- Day 10: Drive to and stay at Tso Moriri, the 'other' lake of Ladakh.
- Day 11: Drive and stay in Jispa or Keylong. You can reach Manali also the same day, but that will mean spending less time admiring the mind-blowing scenery on the way.
- Day 12: Drive to and reach Manali.
- Day 13: From Manali, you can either fly out (from Kullu) or drive to Chandigarh to catch the evening flight.

ITINERARY 2: THE OTHER SIDE OF LADAKH

Category: Road trip plus short trek to Sham Valley, with homestays.

Recommended for: Those visiting Ladakh the second time or for those who want to avoid all the crowded places and see the real Ladakh.

Who can do this: Everyone, basic fitness levels.

How long: 9 days.

When: June to early September.

- Days 1–4: Same as Itinerary 1. You can skip Alchi and save a day here.
- Day 5: Reach Likir, the entry point of Sham Valley, and start the trek.
- Days 5–8: The trek takes you to the villages of Sham Valley which have a network of homestays already established. You stay with the locals and spend time with them. Daily walks are short and easy and rarely last for more than five hours. There is also a road which goes to these villages and you have the choice to sit in the accompanying vehicle if you find the trek too taxing.
- Day 8: The trek ends and you drive back to Leh. Visit Alchi on the way.
- Day 9: Fly out of Leh. Or you can follow Itinerary 1A from here on.

Don't miss—Alchi

Right on the banks of the mighty Indus, the monastery at Alchi is one of its kind and has the best murals you will see anywhere in any Buddhist monastery. Ideally, spend a night in Alchi to truly feel the vibe. This is how Leh used to be before we all wanted to see it.

LOCAL CONTACTS

- Ladakhi Women Travel Company (LWTC) should be the first option for any kind of travel to Ladakh. The first (and only) all-women travel agency in the Indian Himalaya. Contact http://www.ladakhiwomenstravel.com/
- Overland Escape—Amongst the oldest agencies in Leh, it can handle almost all your requirements. Contact http://www.overlandescape.com/

Hand-drawn maps for representation purposes only.
Not to scale.

JOLINGKONG

Where myths are real

The village of Kunthi, in the valley of Vyas, under the mountain of Shiva.

For the most part, Dharchula is a typical small Indian town. Unplanned, dirty, loud and overcrowded. But then, it's also anything but typical. On the banks of the mighty Kali River, across which lies Nepal, and surrounded by huge mountain faces on all sides, it's the starting point of some of the best treks, not just in the Indian Himalaya, but anywhere in the world. The most famous of these treks is to Kailash Mansarovar in Tibet, across the Lipu Lekh Pass. An ancient pilgrimage, beyond parallel. Less popular (but spectacular nonetheless) is the trek to Darma Valley (THE land of flying Lamas from my first book) and even lesser known is the trek to Jolingkong lake. It is a high altitude lake at almost 4,800 metres, right under a peak known locally as 'Adi Kailash' or 'Buddha Kailash', the old Kailash. It is strikingly similar to the Kailash in Tibet and reaching here is nothing short of a pilgrimage, an ode to the wonders of the Himalaya. Just below Jolingkong is the biggest village in the valley, Kuthi, and it takes four days of walking to reach there. Yes, such villages still exist. Just like when we went to Darma Valley in 2008, we were amongst the first group of amateurs to trek there in 2012. And, since then, every trek we have done has been benchmarked against Jolingkong. This is a short account of nine long days of trekking in this locally popular, but otherwise completely unknown land.

A (medical) test and an Army lunch

We reached Dharchula on a hot June afternoon. Yes, it gets hot in the Himalaya too, especially in the towns as they are usually down by the river. The KMVN guesthouse, where we were going to stay the night, had the best possible location, like all government guesthouses do, right on the banks of the Kali and next to the bridge that takes you to Nepal (where we all went that evening). Waiting for us at the guesthouse was Laxman Kutiyal, the person with whom I had coordinated the whole trek.

'Hello sir, I am so excited that we are going to my village,' was the first thing he told me. Kutiyal, referencing 'belonging to Kuthi village' … now I understood. He had been pushing the local government to open the trek to Kuthi and Jolingkong, and finally he had succeeded.

'It's our big festival and Kutiyals from across the state will be coming there. So your timing is very good. But we need to get a medical test done for all participants, it's just a formality,' he added.

'And what if we fail the test?' asked Sangita, who was already having second thoughts about the trek and maybe saw this as a way out.

'Don't think negative, madam,' Laxman replied, which only gave her hope.

So, first thing the next morning, we were at the government clinic to give our urine and blood samples. It was the first time any of us were getting ourselves tested for being 'fit enough to trek'. This is standard procedure for the Kailash Mansarovar trek, and since we would be on the same trek route for the first three days, we had to be medically cleared too. Although we were laughing about it, no one wanted to fail, of course. Not that we even knew what criteria they would use to pass or fail us. In any case, it was the ideal opportunity for Atul to crack jokes related to swapping of urine samples, shaking hands, etc. Once all of us were done, we were told that the results would be out by evening. Our trek was to start early the next morning, so we were cutting it close.

Laxman, though, had full confidence in the test results coming out on time, so we left it to him to take care of. We had somewhere to be after all. A special lunch at the Army camp in Dharchula.

Rajeeb, one of the participants, knew a Major who was posted in Dharchula, and had planned to meet him. The ladies, though, sensed an opportunity to meet the Army men and convinced Rajeeb to tell the Major that he was part of a trek group. The Major was super impressed that we were going to Jolingkong and very graciously invited all of us. So often on our treks, we had passed Army cantonments and had always marvelled at how nice and well-kept they were, and at their discipline in general. And now, we were not just going to see one, we were going to eat a meal there. Sharp at 12.30, three jeeps with smart-looking young soldiers arrived to pick us up. We were escorted to the camp where the Major and his junior officers welcomed us and showed us around. The whole camp was meticulously laid out and well-organised, the officers, intelligent and confident. And we were super proud of the Army all over again. And that was even before we had lunch.

The lunch was delicious, and in typical Army style, served out over four courses. But I remember it much more for the hormonally-charged atmosphere. All the women in our group, and there were quite a few of them, and of all age groups, were on a high. From the way the soldiers looked, to their discipline, fitness and above all, manners, everything led to rapturous 'oohs' and 'aahs'. Not that the soldiers were oblivious to the female attention they were getting. They revelled in it. Finally, reluctant goodbyes were said by both sides, plans made for another lunch after we completed the trek, and we were dropped back at the guesthouse.

'I want to fail the medical test and stay back in Dharchula,' Sarika declared. People were actually sad to leave Dharchula. Who would have thought!

The trek starts

A beaming Laxman delivered the 'good news' that evening. And early next morning we got into local jeeps and started the drive to the roadhead. It was a treacherous drive to say the least. But the super-skilled local drivers ensured that we felt safe. The mountains were taller, the forests wilder and the Kali River more tumultuous. In a couple of hours, we reached the small settlement of Gala, the starting point, at a height of 2,400 metres. Our guides, cooks and horsemen were already there waiting for us. They quickly loaded everything on their horses. It was going to be a long first day and I had prepared everyone as best as I could.

The first day of a trek is always the most mentally challenging. Anyone who has trekked knows that, and any kind of additional physical challenge becomes a big deal. Thankfully, the first 3 km were pretty much on flat trail and put everyone at ease. Not for long though. We reached the spot from where a very steep path led all the way down to the Kali River. A 500-metre drop in less than 2 km. Going down is easy, you must be thinking. It is, but that's not how the human mind works. Everyone was imagining the pain on the last day when we would have to climb this stretch to finish the trek. Check out the picture on page ii of the inserts.

Once we got down though, things got much better. Again, human nature was at play. We quickly forgot what was behind us. And what was ahead was a wide, flat trail along the roaring Kali, all the way to the Day 1 camp at Budhi village (2,700 metres)—one of the advantages of sharing the trail with one of the most popular pilgrimages in the country. It was a long day, almost 16 km, but you can't complain much when it's mostly flat. There were also small dhabas on the way where we had hot lunch, another rarity on a trek in the Indian Himalaya. By 5 p.m., all of us had reached Budhi and had checked into the official camp for the Kailash Mansarovar yatris. Organised by the Army (the Indo-Tibetan Border Police or ITBP), the camp was well-managed and efficient. Everyone was allocated a place to sleep in the bunkers, given blankets and, after dinner, we washed our plates and put them back properly like obedient school kids.

We were sharing the camp with a batch of yatris going to Kailash Mansarovar. Any thoughts we might have entertained about us being great adventurers were quickly put to rest. Here were people, young and old, on their first trip ever to the mountains, with no fancy shoes or backpacks, but doing a difficult trek on sheer faith.

There was a buzz in the camp about the steep climb the next morning, to the meadows of Chialekh. Supposed to be nothing short of magical, the Chialekh meadows were a very important landmark of the trek. Beyond Chialekh, the trail is easy, all the way to Kuthi village.

'Somehow reach Chialekh,' was Laxman's three-word

pep talk to us. We started off next morning with the yatris, hoping to benefit from their energy and faith. It kind of worked. At any point, no matter how tired we felt, there was always someone more tired, less equipped, yet continuing to walk up. We were shamed into not complaining. It was also drizzling constantly, which is always a double-edged sword in the Himalaya. It cools things down, but makes the trail slippery. Slipping, sliding and wet, we managed to reach the forest hut at the top in about three hours. There was an ITBP checkpost and a small dhaba there. It had a fire going.

A long slide to a sinking village

We made full use of the fire—for warmth, to dry our shoes and for hot food. We had climbed almost 500 metres to reach 3,200 metres and everyone was on a high. We were now imagining a stroll in the meadows all the way to our Day 2 campsite. But things are never so straightforward, are they? Laxman broke the news. We would be strolling in the meadows, but just for a couple of kilometres, after which there was a long, steep and extremely slippery path down to the sinking village of Garbyal.

'Wait a minute, a sinking village, as in, it's sinking now?' Duhita, the youngest in the group and the only one excited about what was coming next, asked.

'It's been sinking slowly over the last many years and has been abandoned now. The soil there is like clay. It's a rarest of rare phenomenon,' Laxman replied, with pride. Duhita's excitement rubbed off on us, and forgetting about the perils of the slippery slopes, we took off.

The meadows were amazing, and it was a delight to walk through them after the muddy scramble up. Do check the picture on page ii of the inserts so that I can go straight to the next part. Twice in two days now, we were standing on top of a steep descent. It's difficult to explain what a trekker feels at such moments. It's a mixture of—'at least it's not a climb up + shit, I will have to climb this on the way back + what was the whole point of the previous climb if we have to go down again, this is a useless trek' …

In addition to the above, what we had to contend with was a sight straight from an apocalypse movie. Spread out on the zigzag trail, were our porters and horses, slipping wildly, especially the horses, with some of our luggage scattered along the path. Everyone was shouting and screaming and some young porters were laughing like crazy. The soil was indeed like clay and rain had made it extremely slippery. We froze at the top, till Laxman told us that we were not horses and would not slip as badly, plus there were some porters who would handhold us all the way down. I don't have pictures of what ensued for the next thirty minutes, but it was fun + crazy. After the first couple of times, we got used to slipping and falling. Some of us decided to just sit and slide down as much of the distance as we could. By the time we were down, the rain had stopped and the weather had cleared. We had passed the mountain test.

About twenty minutes later, we reached the first home in Garbyal. It was fascinating. The house had sunk almost till its windows, which by the way had excellent wood work. This was true for the entire village. All the homes had sunk to different levels, some almost till the roofs, and they all sported beautiful carvings.

'It was a village of traders, very rich, and they displayed their wealth through wood carvings,' we were told. The people must have been flashy and adventurous, but not very good at identifying a solid base to build their homes. The picture is on page ii of the inserts.

The valley of Vyas

Our Day 2 halt was in the village of Napalchu (3,200 metres), on the banks of the Kali, across which was Gunji village, the halt for Kailash yatris. So technically, we had separated from them. No more ITBP camps for us now. Just ahead, the Kali took a right turn and the Kailash trail would follow it. And we would follow the Kuthi River that flowed in from the left.

In Napalchu, we stayed in a local house, two-storied, like they all are, made of wood and stone. The host was an old man and from the moment we reached, he wanted us to drink chang, the local home-made brew, mostly as an excuse so that he could drink some himself. We wanted to settle down, relax and eat something, but the man was insistent. We finally had a couple of sips each and it was all that he needed to down his own glass and then one more. He was content afterwards. We had a good time in the house, and a decent sleep (you can't hope for more when twelve people are sleeping in a room).

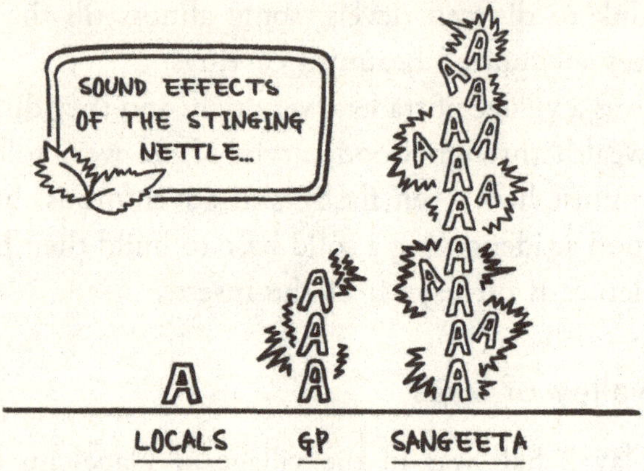

THE STINGING NETTLE

Bichhu buti, as it's locally called, is a wild thorny bush that grows across the high Himalaya. Anyone who has trekked will have some experience of accidentally touching it, and recoiling in sharp stinging pain. It lasts for about thirty minutes and numbs you. According to the locals though, it's just a mild pain, so mild that the nettles are used by parents to discipline their kids. Apart from that, they make delicious soup and chutney from it and also use it as a pain killer. The old man insisted that if we hit our knees or ankles with bichhu buti, all our aches would disappear. We had nothing better to do and my knee was actually hurting, so I volunteered. Ganesh, my guide of so many treks, didn't give me a chance to reconsider my decision and bombarded my knee with multiple blows even before I could let out the first scream. It hurt like hell. But so strong was my resolve to see the others suffer, that

> I pretended to be just mildly uncomfortable. Sangita took the bait and her cries shook the foundations of the old house. After that, it was almost mandatory for everyone to get a beating and Ganesh swung away wildly. We were mortally afraid of bichhu buti for the rest of the trek.

• • •

After Day 2, the trail became relaxed, and the views became clearer. There were two full rainbows in the sky, something was special—we had entered the Byans Valley. Rishi Vyas supposedly hailed from this valley and wrote the *Mahabharata* in these mountains. *Mahabharata* legends are spread across the entire Himalaya, but here, they are more intense. Up ahead were the ruins of an old fort, which is locally known as Pandava Killa. Our destination for the day was the biggest village of the valley, the Kuthi village, home of Kunthi, mother of the Pandavas. It was another long day of trekking, but so beautiful was the landscape that even the habitual complainers, Sarika and Sangita, were quiet. Gigantic mountain faces, snow- covered peaks, the crystal clear waters of the Kuthi, the flat trail passing through meadows and pastures, shepherds and their herds … it was the whole Himalayan thing condensed into one day. It was therapeutic trekking.

We were on the trail for more than ten hours, when one last bend around the mountain and voila, the stunning—for lack of words—Kuthi. Sitting pretty under a mighty mountain covered in snow, the slate-covered roofs shining in the afternoon light, was this most magical place we had ever seen. You can see the first view of Kuthi on page iii of the inserts. Partly overwhelmed by the fact that the day's trek was almost over, but mostly by its sheer beauty, we picked up pace so as to reach there quicker. But you know what is coming right—it is never as easy as it looks. The trail seemed flat, but there were at least four places where it went down to cross a stream and then climbed back up again. We had estimated thirty minutes for the last two kilometres and it took us one-and-a-half excruciating hours.

But Kuthi was every bit as special from up close as it was from far away. To add to the special feeling, it was buzzing with activity. Kutiyals from far and near were there for the annual gathering, and it was a festive atmosphere. To top it all, we had a rest day the next day. No trekking, maybe a bath, and lots and lots of festival food. This, while staying in this legendary village at 3,500 metres, surrounded by high mountains and the warm sun. No one tells you about such joys on a trek. And they can't be told either. They have to be experienced.

A day in Kuthi

It was the fourth day of our trek, a day which we had looked forward to on the tiring stretches. A rest day. A full day of doing nothing. It started with Laxman announcing arrangements for a hot water bath. After four days of 'no bath', a hot water bath acquires a different meaning and counts way above any luxury you can think of. But before that, it was time to answer nature's call. I am going into these details because they need to be told. Laxman led all of us through the village, with its narrow lanes and beautiful homes, to the outskirts, where there was a small stream. Its water was diverted to a small tank and there were four toilets ahead. The entire village used these toilets and took turns to keep them clean. This was 'Swacch Bharat' before the slogan came into being. It was a first on any of our treks, and since then, I have seen this system only in a village in Darma Valley in 2016. Anyway, it was a delightful experience and a relieved bunch walked back, chatting with the villagers.

Post the hot shower (oh, it was so amazing), we were all set for the first round of festival food. We had puris made from kuttu ka atta, buckwheat, a specialty of this valley and something that is supposed to have given Rishi Vyas all the intelligence and wisdom to write the *Mahabharata*. This was served with mustard raita, and it is a taste I haven't forgotten till date. Breakfast merged into lunch and all we did was eat whatever was given to us. There were local green vegetables, dal, nettle chutney (so, it was true) and sweets. Then we had an afternoon nap.

The late afternoon sun was delightfully warm and we went for a walk in the village. Some old women were sitting on the roofs of their homes, soaking in the sun (they always do in the Himalaya) and invited us up. On we went to the slate rooftop, and sat and chatted. They were concerned about what would happen to their village after they were gone, as the young people were moving to Dharchula and beyond for higher education and then jobs. This is a predicament most of the high Himalayan villages are facing. An entire way of life is at the cusp of being extinguished.

It wasn't like this always. Before 1962, this region was on a thriving trade route between Kumaon and Tibet. In fact, at Jolingkong, there used to be a year-round Tibetan market and traders from everywhere would visit. The war changed everything, and overnight, the villagers here lost their means of livelihood. It's the same story across the entire length of the Indian Himalaya, along the border with Tibet.

They were not sad though—they never are. They have seen enough of life to not be. Also, there was hope that the almost-deserted village would get a new lease of life as the Army had proposed to build a road all the way till Kuthi. They were hopeful that the village would soon be full of young men and women, and children. In the meanwhile, they entertained themselves by cracking jokes with the funny ones in our group—Atul and VJ. Atul complimented them on their good looks and good skin and asked them the secret, '… for VJ,' he said. They pointed at the mountain behind us and told him to climb it to get the special herb which they use to stay young forever. It was an unscalable mountain, with a straight rock face. Atul looked at it and realised that he had been well played. One of the ladies and her daughter Sheela, who had come from Dharchula on her pony (she rode her most of the way), invited us to their house and we gladly accepted. These were more than 300-year-old homes, and we had always wondered how they look inside.

Dark. That's how they looked. Dark and cosy. For

protection from the cold is the main aim of these houses. The stone and wood act as insulators, the tiny windows and doors let in minimum cold and light. But your eyes soon adjust. We went in with them into their kitchen, which is always the hub of the house. We were guests, so she gave us chakti, the home-made beer, which we had while sitting around the chulha and warming ourselves. She then gave us an option of local butter chai or 'normal' chai, which was served from a Milton flask which they had bartered for five blankets in Tibet. Sheela's pony, the bartered flask, yes, these were real things.

We had a great time at their house and it was soon time to go back and pack for the next day. We were to take only the things we needed and keep the rest of the stuff behind. Tomorrow was the day we would reach Jolingkong. The sky was dark with clouds, and soon it started snowing, capping a wonderful day in Kuthi.

Jolingkong

Morning dawned nice and bright. The village and the surrounding mountains were under a carpet of fresh snow, which started to melt as soon as the sun came out. It was a perfect day for trekking, and our bodies and minds were well-rested. Off we went. But in just about twenty minutes, we were breathless and exhausted, and it was all back to normal. It was a relentless climb the whole time, sometimes steep sometimes easy, but uphill always. We met some locals who were either going or returning from Jolingkong. It was a holy place for them. They were accompanied either by their horses (the lead horse being totally decked up) or dzos (a cross between a yak and a cow).

Close to 4,000 metres and midway to Jolingkong, we reached a beautiful open pasture. A shepherd from Kangra (it is really a long way from here) had camped there with his sheep and he was happy to share the meadow with us. Our cook was in a good mood, and along with lunch, he made us tea as well. As we sipped hot tea, ate our meal and appreciated the beauty all around us, the clouds parted and revealed Adi Kailash. We were mesmerised, speechless and overwhelmed. Here is the first view of Adi Kailash, on page iii of the inserts.

The rest of the walk was completed in a daze. We constantly looked up at the mountain, at its beautiful form. Laxman told us that this was an extremely lucky sighting, as Adi Kailash is always behind clouds and rarely reveals itself. We were sure that what we were seeing was special. We crossed some snow patches, more meadows and finally reached the ITBP (yes, the good old Army was here as well) base camp at 4,500 metres. By evening, the Adi Kailash was back behind clouds, but none of us complained. We had had our fill.

It was amongst the highest campsites on a trek anywhere in the world, and by 6 p.m., it was impossible to stand outside. It was bitterly cold and we were further in awe of the Indian Army for just always being there. They had warm beds, blankets, good food and lots of smiles for us. We were well-acclimatised too, and none of us faced any altitude-related problems. We had a restful, if not uninterrupted sleep.

The next morning, we climbed a little higher, first to the legendary rice fields of Jolingkong (rice actually grows at this altitude, check the picture on page iii of the inserts) and then finally to the lake at 4,700 metres. It is a large, quiet lake and we spent an hour just sitting and staring, lost in our thoughts. Then it was time for pictures and the long journey back. Return journeys on a trek are filled with many emotions; of knowing what lies ahead, of missing what has been left behind, of the anticipation of familiar comforts and of slowly disengaging from the life that has been led over the last few days.

Some quick highlights

Another long stop at the meadow with the shepherd before reaching Kuthi for the night. Then an unplanned lunch with some village women working in the fields. They shared their rice and dal, we gladly accepted (we never say no). Laughter and jokes on trails where we were struggling to stay alive, just two days ago. A night at Napalchu and we indulged the old man there by sharing his drink. Passed the sinking village of Garbyal ('How much has it sunk since we passed?' Duhita wanted to know) and climbed the not-slippery-anymore trail to Chialekh. Said our byes to the jawans posted at the checkpost of Chialekh and climbed down to Budhi village, this time, staying in a homestay. It took us three days from Jolingkong, but it is just a blur now.

THE TALE OF ANOTHER LAKE

There are about 4,699 high altitude lakes in the Indian Himalaya as per an ISRO study in 2013. These are lakes above the altitude of 3,000 metres. Four thousand, six hundred and ninety-nine. You would think that, with so much to explore, trekkers would have their hands full. Not if you see the long queues leading up to the Roopkund during season.

It's a fascinating study in human behaviour. Once a high, remote, mysterious Himalayan pond, Roopkund has now become one of the most-trodden trails in the Indian Himalaya. This transition can be attributed to many things—easy availability of information about trekking, cheap trekking options (sometimes at the cost of trek ethics and ecological sensitivity), sharing of your 'achievements' on social media, concentrated young working population in some urban centres and their need to break free of the routine. But whatever the reason, the end result is that, every year for the past few years, hundreds, if not thousands, are trekking to Roopkund. The last time 'adventure seekers' showed such enthusiasm for a trek, it led to the destruction and subsequent closure of the Valley of Flowers. What awaits Roopkund?

• • •

The final climb

And just like that, we were on the final day of the trek and at the last stretch. The 500-metre climb. Since morning, everyone had psyched themselves about the climb and now it was upon us, and we had nowhere to go but up. And up we went. Panting and cursing, huffing and puffing. The mid-day sun was harsh and there was no respite. Trekking felt like the cruellest thing in the world. The locals kept passing us, offering sympathetic looks, nothing more. Some of us lay sprawled on the railing, some on all fours, and some just lay in the middle of the trail. It felt like this would never end. But then came divine intervention. Who else, but the Army. There was a small paltan of soldiers going back to Dharchula, and as they passed us, they offered kind encouragements. It was a matter of pride for the women who had been lusting after the soldiers, just a few days ago. And when one of them said, 'Mataji, you can do it', to Sangita, it was like a collective jolt to their egos. Second and third wind appeared in quick succession and the climb was completed with clenched teeth and fists.

Another 3 km on a flat stretch and we saw the wonderful sight of cars waiting to take us back. Nine days, 150 km, 2,400 metres of climbing and back, not counting the numerous ups and downs in between. But these are just numbers. What can't be counted are the emotions invested, the moments shared, the feelings experienced, the difficulties, the triumphs, the bonding, the disconnect from the rest of the world and the connection to the self. Oh trekking, there is nothing like you.

P.S.: We reached Dharchula on a high which was partially deflated by the news that the Major had to leave for the plains, so lunch wouldn't happen. However, a promise is a promise. We were asked our vehicle number and time of departure from Dharchula. Midway on the long road back to Kathgodam, a rendezvous was set up. As we approached the point, an Army Gypsy was spotted coming from the other side. The reunion with the Major happened in the middle of the road and we exchanged snacks and laughter.

THE GUIDE

Since this is the only story from Kumaon, I will take the opportunity to give out some itineraries that will help you explore this beautiful region. In summer, when the neighbouring Garhwal gets overrun by the Char Dham pilgrims, Kumaon retains its sanity and is a much better option to spend your vacation. The middle region of Kumaon has some really nice places to stay and chill, and do things like birding, cycling, camping, etc. Further north are some of the most spectacular treks.

ITINERARY 3: A SHORT TRIP TO KUMAON

Category: Road trip plus short walks.

Recommended for: Those who are short on time but want a quick getaway to the hills.

Who can do this: Everyone, age and fitness levels no bar.

How long: 5 days.

When: Through the year.

- Day 1: Fly into Pantnagar or take a train to Kathgodam. From there, within a drive of three hours, there are many places you can reach. For example:

  Sonapani: To chill amidst fruit orchards and enjoy the views.

  Jilling: For bird-watching enthusiasts.

  Binsar: For staying in an old colonial bungalow in a pristine forest.
- Day 2, 3 and 4: Spend at your chosen location. Go out for short walks, etc.
- Day 5: Drive back to Pantnagar / Kathgodam for flight / train.

ITINERARY 4:
A SUMMER IN KUMAON

Category: Road trip combined with a short trek.

Recommended for: Ideal summer vacation with family.

Who can do this: Everyone, basic fitness levels.

How long: 8 days.

When: May to June.

- Day 1: Fly into Pantnagar or take a train to Kathgodam. Drive to and reach a midway place like Binsar or Mukteshwar.
- Day 2: Continue the drive and reach Kausani or Vijaypur for the night. We are taking it easy so that you are not overwhelmed by the road trip, and also, so that you don't miss out on the journey for the destination.
- Day 3: Reach Munsiyari. Your base for the next three days. It has good options to stay and unbelievable views of the Pancha Chuli peaks.
- Day 4: Rest and walk around Munsiyari.
- Day 5: Trek to Khaliya Top. 6 km uphill walk, but the fascinating views from the top are worth every step. Camp there for the night.
- Day 6: After an easy morning at the top, walk back to Munsiyari.

- Day 7: Return journey starts. Reach midway place like Binsar or Almora.
- Day 8: Start early and reach Kathgodam to catch the train back.

ITINERARY 5: (A, B AND C)—TREKKING IN KUMAON

Category: Trek

Recommended for: Those looking for a proper Himalayan trek.

Who can do this: Anyone willing to step out of their comfort zone and who has good fitness levels.

How long: 9 to 13 days.

When: June, September and October.

ITINERARY 5A: NANDA DEVI EAST BASE CAMP TREK

Category: Medium grade and long.

- Days 1–3: Same as Itinerary 4.
- Day 4–11: Start the trek to Nanda Devi east base camp via Martoli village. It's an eight-day trek

back and forth, one of the longest in the Indian Himalaya.

- Day 11: Back in Munsiyari after the trek.
- Day 12: Return journey starts. Reach midway place like Binsar or Almora.
- Day 13: Start early and reach Kathgodam to catch the train back.

ITINERARY 5B: DARMA VALLEY TREK

Category: Easy and shorter. Everyone can do.

- Day 1: Fly into Pantnagar or take a train to Kathgodam. Drive to and reach a midway place like Binsar or Mukteshwar.
- Day 2: Drive and reach Pithoragarh, second night stop.
- Day 3: Drive and reach Dharchula, the base of Darma Valley trek.
- Days 4–8: Trek to Darma Valley now starts from Nagling village as the road has almost reached there. Go to Pancha Chuli base camp and back. Then a day's walk to the meadows of Nagling and back.
- Day 8: Reach Dharchula by late morning and drive further to a midway place like Binsar or Almora.
- Day 9: Start early and reach Kathgodam to catch the train back.

ITINERARY 5C: JOLINGKONG TREK

Category: Medium grade and long.

- Days 1-3: Same as 5B
- Days 4-9: Trek to Jolingkong. There is road network in between now, which shortens the trek by a couple of days.
- Day 10: Reach Dharchula by late morning and drive further to a midway place like Binsar or Almora.
- Day 11: Start early and reach Kathgodam to catch the train back.

Don't miss—Patal Bhubaneshwar

Set your fears aside and enter this underground cave which surely must count as one of the natural wonders of the world. The locals regard it very highly, but even if religious mythology is not your thing, this is worth every minute you drive to reach there, simply as a natural phenomenon.

LOCAL CONTACTS

1. Ganesh Jangpani of Munsiyari—For any trek around Munsiyari, he is my tried and tested guide for a decade now. Contact 9720814252 / 9997646952.
2. Laxman Kutiyal of Kuthi—For any trek starting from Dharchula. Contact 9458858335 / 9968276771.
3. Bobby from Kathgodam for all your transportation needs. Contact 9410588889.

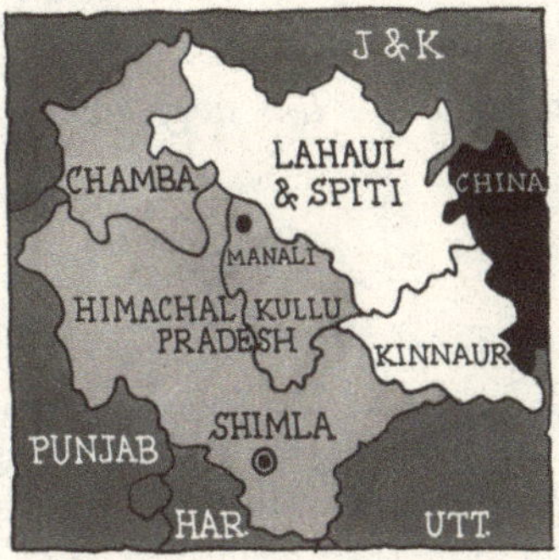

Hand-drawn maps for representation purposes only.
Not to scale.

SPITI

Stranded in Pin Valley

Sometimes, one trip provides you with a lifetime of stories. In 2006, Rujuta and I drove to Kinnaur, and from there, trekked into Spiti over the 4,900-metres high Pin Bhabha Pass connecting the Bhabha Valley in Kinnaur with the Pin Valley in Spiti. We were blown away by the sheer magnitude of the Himalaya and the raw beauty of the meadows, the glaciers, the high plateau before the pass, our campsites, everything. It's relatively crowded these days, but in 2006, we were the only humans (apart from our cook, horseman and porter) in the entire region for the four days of the trek. I wrote about the adventurous pass crossing on the third day of the trek in The Land of Flying Lamas, *in which I had also talked about our encounter with the 'friendly spirit'. This story picks up from there.*

After our encounter with the friendly spirit, we crossed the Pin Bhabha Pass, walked down the glacier, then the moraine and camped at Phaldar. The trek, something that had occupied our mind space for the last three months, was effectively over. All that remained was to walk to Mudh village and start the second phase of our Spiti trip.

'It's a straight walk, sir, not like yesterday. We will walk along the Pin River, and will be in Mudh by 2 p.m. Your car will be waiting for you there,' declared a confident Gatuk.

And so we started the next morning, our team of Rujuta and me, Gatuk, Lobzang and Kalu, and the four donkeys (two white and two black). We walked the 'last day of trek walk'—easy, confident steps, appreciating the landscape, soaking in the achievement. After crossing the Pin River over a small bridge, we climbed onto the track which had been recently cut as a possible road across the Pin Bhabha Pass to Kinnaur. While Gatuk and Lobzang were against the laying of the road (their livelihood was this trek), Kalu was hoping that it would get made as it would be easier for the people from his village to reach Kinnaur. Connectivity in the remote Himalaya is a complicated choice between access and preservation.

'Sir, dekho, "pink river",' Gatuk broke our train of thought. We looked at where he was pointing across the river, and even amidst the pastel shades of the Pin Valley, it was clearly visible. A bed of pink stones, snaking down a side valley, in between brown and purple mountains, just like a river would. But not a river, more like a moraine. Tough to describe it, so check the picture on page iv of the inserts.

We were all walking together, talking and laughing, aware that, after a few hours, we would be going our separate ways. The donkeys were ahead of us, eager to reach Mudh now that they sensed its proximity.

'They will stop straight in Mudh now,' declared Lobzang, and like the proverbial 'spoken too soon', just as we rounded the bend, there they were in the distance, not moving, just standing.

'It's the first stream,' Gatuk said. 'But why have they stopped? They can just jump over it.'

And just like that, we were in the middle of our second adventure in two days.

A night by the stream

Lobzang ran ahead, and all of us quickened our pace to see what had happened. As we got closer, we heard the rush of water. It was the stream. Usually a gentle brook, sometimes even a trickle, it had turned into a roaring torrent, blowing away the stone embankment which had never been tested before.

'I have never seen this in my lifetime,' Gatuk said. Kalu and Lobzang agreed.

'Where is this water coming from?'

We got the answer a day later, but for you, dear reader, this is what had happened. While we had enjoyed almost perfect weather over the last few days on the trek, there had been flash floods in the Pin Valley of Spiti, which had caused heavy landslides, swept away bridges and roads, stranded locals and tourists alike, and had even killed a few. It was an unprecedented, unheard of, unplanned for disaster. It's not supposed to rain here, let alone a cloudburst. Textbooks teach us that it's a cold desert / rain shadow / arid region. But here it was, crumbling under the water. Once again, we were seeing the remote Himalayan regions and its people suffering from changing climate patterns while the world debates.

At that moment, however, we were just clueless. Our first and only thought was, how were we to cross the stream? In the last three days on the trek, we must have crossed more than a dozen streams. But they were crossable, none of them had been flooded, with water and rocks thundering down.

For the next two hours, we tried all means; we went upstream, then downstream, formed a chain, went solo, but were thwarted every time. We couldn't even reach the middle of the stream, nor could we find a good place to cross it. Finally, after a sustained attempt, Kalu, the strongest of the lot, was able to cross over. But the first thing he shouted from the other side was 'don't attempt, too dangerous'. It was quickly decided that we needed help, so Kalu was to run to the village, get some people along and help us cross over. Till then, we would wait.

It was noon when we sat on the track beside the stream and started our wait. The donkeys went grazing, Gatuk and Lobzang were chatting, and Rujuta and I were staring ahead at the beautiful Pin Valley. We could see miles ahead, a unique characteristic of the trans-Himalaya. We weren't necessarily worried, not yet. I mean you do expect something like this when you go for a high Himalayan trek. But you are with guides, the trek staff, and they know what is to be done.

'Lunch kha lo sir, he will take at least two to three hours.'

Yup, food is hope and strength, and we needed it.

Five hours later, we were still waiting. With every passing hour, our chances of reaching Mudh that day had nosedived. The water in the stream had increased after the afternoon melt of the glaciers above and we would need considerable help from Kalu and his friends to cross it now. Admirably, we were patient, quite aware of the fact that there was really not much we could do. Our donkeys, though, were not so patient. They kept trying their luck, and their futile attempts provided us with some much-needed distraction. At around 5 p.m., we saw a thunderstorm in the distance, dark clouds and what looked like streaks of rain below them. It was a fascinating sight, especially their slow crawl towards us.

'Sir, tent pitch karna padega,' Gatuk stated the obvious. Without saying it out aloud, everyone knew that we were spending the night there.

Just as we crawled inside our tent, we heard the pitter-patter of rain outside. It was light, but consistent, the high Himalayan rain. When the stomach started grumbling, we realised we hadn't eaten much since lunch.

'Gatuk, dinner ka scene?' I shouted from the tent.

'Sir, food almost over, thoda dal chawal, bas,' came the reply.

We had a quick dinner during a break in the rain, and discussed our plan of action. And this is what was decided—we would wake at 4 a.m. and try to cross the stream when it had the least amount of water (glaciers freeze during the night). It sounded like a sensible plan, and if the weather was clear, we would be able to make the crossing without much trouble. Then we said good night and were back in the tent, trying to sleep. All I remember of that night was feeling hungry and checking my watch every hour.

Donkeys go missing, dog comes chasing

We were up much before 4 a.m., but waited for Gatuk and Lobzang to come out of their tent before we got out of ours. It was bitterly cold and dark outside. As we packed our stuff and put on our shoes, we saw Lobzang running around frantically and waving his hands.

'What happened?'

'Sir, gadhe bhaag gaye.'

The two black donkeys (the 'chaalu' ones) must have figured out about the water level being low early in the morning, just like we did, and crossed over and run to Mudh. Without the luggage they were supposed to carry.

So now, not only did we have to cross the stream, we would have to carry the luggage too. Gatuk decided that it was time for some sacrifice. He and Lobzang would help me and Rujuta cross over, and they would stay back till Kalu brought help.

'Let's go, no time to think.' And then we stepped inside the coldest water ever.

We formed a chain—Lobzang, Rujuta and Gatuk, and me in the end. We stumbled, almost tumbled, then fumbled (for the guide's hand when we lost our grip), and after a heroic struggle for forty-five minutes (by the guides) in the dim light of the stars and the light from our head torches, we crossed over. Gatuk and Lobzang turned back mid-stream when the tough stretch was over. Rujuta and I somehow managed to reach the bank and threw ourselves on dry land. What must explorers feel after climbing mountains and crossing oceans, when the elation we felt after wading through thigh-high water for 30 feet was this high, I thought out aloud.

'Abe saale, it's freezing, we have to move.'

Rujuta, the practical Maharashtrian, wasted no time in feelings of joy and things like that. We got up, looked back at the stream and at Gatuk and Lobzang on the other side waving at us and smiling, and started walking.

Never had we felt this tiny and insignificant as we did that day, walking in that surreal landscape with our backpacks, the scale of the mountains and the Pin River dwarfing us and our egos. And never will we (hopefully) forget this lesson of insignificance in the grand scheme of things. It was still very early and therefore very cold, and on top of that, we were drenched. After some time, when she couldn't take it anymore, Rujuta stopped in the middle of the trail, took off her tracks and changed into dry ones.

'Now it's better, let's go.'

I didn't even get a chance to contemplate doing the same, it was that quick. And on we went, looking around in awe and wonder.

'Woof, woof, woof.'

A distant barking, almost like a growl, broke the deafening silence of the last thirty minutes.

'What is that?'

We looked around but could see nothing.

'Woof.'

'It has to be a sheep dog,' I reasoned, 'but where?'

We scanned the landscape. No movement. Unknowingly, we quickened our pace.

'Woof, woof.'

Not so distant now. Closing in.

'Sheep dogs don't bite, right,' one of us asked the other.

'Not unless threatened.'

And did we pose a threat? God knows.

'Woof, woof, woof.' It sounded much closer, almost on top of us.

'Shit, look up,' and from the mountain above, a big brown sheep dog was coming straight towards us, slowly but steadily.

We could have mistaken it for a bear from that distance, but the barbed wire around its neck gave it away. Sheep dogs in the higher Himalaya are a sight to behold. Huge, with a thick coat of fur and lion-like mane, they can take on a leopard single-handedly, protected as they are from the lethal bite by the wire around their necks. Not your average domesticated dog (don't pet them), they are regal creatures, and very much like to be on their own, minding their business, unless of course, you are a threat to the sheep. And that was the thought flashing across our minds as we watched it mesmerised—how were we a threat? We couldn't even see the sheep!

'Keep walking, it will go away,' I whispered, hoping and praying. While still looking back we started walking briskly, me trying hard to keep my deep-rooted fear of dogs in control. The dog was getting nearer, sounding and looking very angry.

'I have never heard of a sheep dog attacking trekkers,' Rujuta tried to reassure me. But it was not about ever, it was about now, and right now he was closing in. He came right above the trail, and in one big leap, landed just about ten feet from us. For a long time both of us stared at him—the dog growling, us trying to breathe.

He then started walking slowly towards us, snarling and looking menacing. Instinctively, I bent down and picked up a stone. He stopped.

'Don't throw the stone at him,' Rujuta warned.

'Not at him, but close by, just to scare him. There is no other choice if he comes any nearer.' He did. And I did. It backed off. And we did too. Somehow we held ourselves from running, just walking fast, hoping that he would not come after us. But he resumed his chase. In about five minutes, he was close enough for me to repeat the stone-throwing act, buying us some time again to move on. The trail was winding, and after every turn, I looked back, hoping against hope that he would not be there. But like it happens in horror movies, he reappeared around each bend, determined to get us. This sequence played itself out for more than an hour, exhausting us mentally, much more than crossing the stream had. And just when we were about to totally lose it, he wasn't there. And, it was over.

A village on pause

We kept glancing back for the next half an hour or so, unwilling to believe he wasn't there anymore. Were we in his territory? Had his sheep been harmed in the rain? Where was the shepherd? We kept discussing these things through the rest of the trip. But at that moment, our thoughts moved to the second stream. If the first one was flooded, the second one would be too. And without the help of our guides, how were we to cross it? Two un-crossable, flooded streams separated us from our guides and Mudh village. Suddenly the relief we had felt after the dog disappeared, vanished. But not for long. As we rounded one of the bends, we were greeted by a sight that we cherish till date. Kalu and a guy were walking towards us.

Kalu was delighted to see us too. We told him about the sheep dog and he told us about the flooded second stream.

'But not worry, Nobjung take you.'

'And you?'

He was going to go help his friends pack the stuff and cross the first stream. We said a quick bye and immediately started walking with Nobjung. He was a shy, strong Spitian, and although he smiled every time we spoke to him, he didn't say much. Soon, we saw Mudh village, and within fifteen minutes, were right next to the stream. Nobjung took one look at the flooded stream, one look at both of us, and announced—'Madam, aap meri peeth pe.' Then he looked at me and told me to walk right behind him, holding Rujuta's backpack and placing my feet exactly where he placed his. He looked in total control of the situation. Kalu had brought the expert.

With Rujuta enjoying a joy ride and I playing the 'blind follower' role to perfection, we had a relatively easier crossing.

Two women welcomed us on the other side. Gatuk's mother and wife. His mother couldn't speak a word of Hindi but she communicated so much with her gestures, her smile and her eyes. She was worried for Gatuk; she now knew that he was safe, but would certainly feel better once he was home. The unheard of rains and flooding, the devastation it had caused, had ruffled her. She took our hands and climbed up the steep slope to the village, an utterly exhausting exercise for us, but not a breath out of place for her. And finally, after a full twenty-four hours later than we were supposed to, we entered Mudh village. (A picture of Mudh village from a later trip, on page iv of the inserts.)

I will always remember the short walk from the stream to Gatuk's home. It was just like in the movies.

You know, when everything around you pauses or goes in slow motion, but you are moving at normal speed. Men drinking tea paused with their cups midway, Israeli trekkers playing cards froze, hands in mid-air, children playing football stopped, the ball rolling away as they stared at us. We tried smiling and waving. Nothing, no response. We were cold and tired at that moment so we decided to decode this later. First, we needed food and a warm place.

Gatuk's mother and sister led the way, while persistently offering to carry our backpacks. Nobjung was behind us. We entered their house from the ground floor and then climbed up a flight of stairs to the kitchen, and to instant warmth. Oh, you must experience a Spiti or Ladakhi kitchen when it's cold outside.

THE SPITI KITCHEN

Much like the Ladakhi, and in fact the entire trans-Himalayan area, the kitchen here is the centre of the house. The warmest, cleanest, most spacious part of the house and the best-equipped. This kitchen was typical. A large square room with the 'bukhari' in the middle and a mud pipe rising from it to act as a chimney. One whole wall had shelves with crockery neatly arranged on them; another had other utensils. All rations were kept in an attached store room.

We sat on seats made of thick blankets that had been kept along two walls of the room. The bukhari was continuously fed with fuel and was the source of all the warmth that was making us feel so much better. Warmth is precious for Spitians. Everything is designed to keep as much of it inside as possible. Mud walls, cattle on the ground floor and layers of hand-woven blankets. This is what helps them survive the bitterly cold and long winters, when the mercury drops to -25 degrees C. Plus of course, the 'arak', the alcohol brewed at home, from barley.

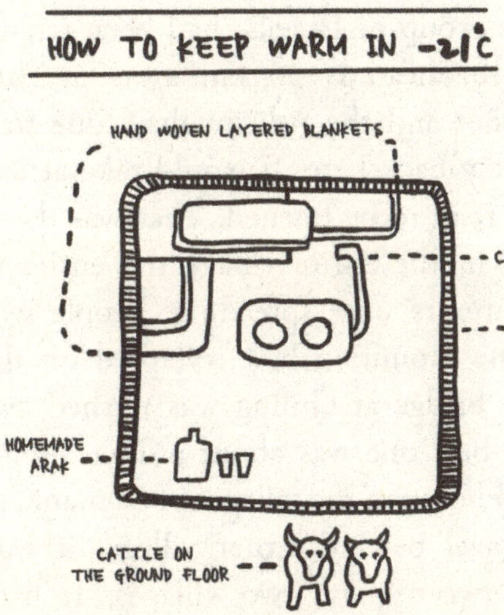

• • •

The view from the small window of the kitchen was spectacular. The pastel shades of the mountains, the raging Pin River, the clouds … all combined to make it appear like a painting. We were offered some butter tea and then some more. And then a plateful of thick omelette, the thickest we had ever seen, tasting not really like what we had ever eaten. But hunger overpowers taste and we devoured it (although it left a permanent impression on our taste buds and we have never since viewed an omelette the same way again). Well-fed, hydrated and warm, we were now ready to listen.

Gatuk's wife told us that the village and the entire Pin Valley had been cut off from the main Spiti Valley for almost six days. Many locals and some trekkers, including the group of Israelis, had been stranded there. The nearest roadhead is 30 km away at Attargu, but the bad weather and the risk involved due to landslides made them stay back here. It would take at least a week more for the road to be opened. That was the only topic of discussion in the entire village the entire time. And obviously, rumours were spreading. People were talking about how the mountain had collapsed on the road or how the new bridge at Guling was washed away within seconds. The best one was about a Tata Sumo that had been stranded between the villages of Sagnam and Tailing. Unable to travel beyond either village, it was ferrying passengers between these two villages. It had attained almost a mythical status. (I really liked this one, and was secretly hoping for it to be true.)

Before we could process this information, Gatuk's mother, who had been sitting by the window looking outside the whole time, turned around and said, 'Aa gaya.' We all went to the window, and despite scanning the scene outside to the best of our abilities, couldn't make out anything or anyone. But she could. After ten more minutes passed, we saw a group of three men walking on the track, a long way off. They were no more than specks, so how had the old woman spotted them? Gatuk's wife told us that her mother-in-law had looked out of this window all her life and it was like a painting for her, in which she could spot the tiniest change.

The escape

Gatuk and company reached home an hour later and a happy family reunion followed. Rujuta and I went out for a walk in the village and told everyone our story, and listened to theirs. During the short time that we spent talking to the villagers and other trekkers, it became clear that no one knew anything for sure. Including the condition of the road to Attargu. While I could relate to how everyone in the village was waiting it out and not trying, let's say, to walk to Attargu, Rujuta obviously couldn't.

'We have already lost a day, let's not just sit here. Let's try to at least go as far as we can.'

'Okay, let's talk to Gatuk and everyone and see what they feel,' I replied, though I was not sure.

Surprisingly, they were open to the suggestion. Gatuk felt that we were well-acclimatised and could surely try. According to Kalu, if the weather improved, we could leave in the morning and walk till it was safe, and then take a call. There were villages along the way where we could stay if needed.

'But we don't know anyone,' I said.

'But I do,' he replied sheepishly.

'You are coming with us!' we both shouted excitedly.

'Yes, I need to go to Kaza too.'

This was great news. With Kalu along, our chances increased manifold. And even better news, Lobzang also was to walk with us till his village. So it was decided that we would leave at 7 a.m. and take it as it comes. It was thrilling—we felt like real adventurers.

We left early the next morning, and walking steadily on the road, reached our first stop, Tailing, in a couple of hours. This was Lobzang's village and he insisted that we go to his house. We couldn't understand why he wanted us to take a diversion, even if it was a short one, when we had so far to go. But he was insistent and told us that there was an alternate route, a walking trail from his village, parallel to the road. We agreed (we were hungry too, and he promised good food) and availed the hospitality of yet another Spitian home.

When we were about to leave, Lobzang came out of his room after a change of clothes, with a bag on his shoulder. He was coming with us too! He said he had nothing better to do and what we were doing was brave and exciting. The more the merrier. And we got back on the trail.

We were now in the land of the mythical Tata Sumo. My eyes scanned the distance for any sign of it. Although we were not on the main road, we could still see it. And just then, a white speck came on the horizon … the Tata Sumo. We shouted and pointed to the car, which was for real. It was on its way to Tailing, and by the time it came back, we would have reached Sagnam on foot, anyway. So we moved on, feeling lighter in our hearts and strangely very hopeful.

Our plan was to cover the distance in two days and take a break at Guling. But we made good time and reached there by 2 p.m. The road till there was not bad, with just a few stretches which were difficult. We stopped at a shabby-looking dhaba and had some noodles, the only food available. The locals told us that it was a further four-hour walk, and that the road would get quite bad. But some people had made their way across from Attargu that morning, so we knew it could be negotiated. We were not really tired, we had two strong guys with us for support, there was going to be daylight for another five hours, and we felt quite optimistic—the decision was a foregone conclusion. We would walk.

As soon as we left the village, we came across a series of landslides and gradually realised that the whole mountainside had actually collapsed on the road. There was no road left. We were walking on the debris where the road used to be. The Pin River was flowing ever so menacingly close, much above the danger mark. Small stones were rolling down the mountainside. The ground below our feet was shaking, or maybe we were. But it was nerve-racking. Kalu took charge and told us to walk in single file and quietly follow him. No one was to speak (or sneeze), as even the slightest disturbance could trigger a landslide. And so we walked for almost an hour, just blindly following him, all the enthusiasm of the morning drained out, focusing just on the next step and not letting ourselves think too much. At one place, there was a huge hole in the middle of the road. A small stream of water coming down the mountain was swirling and going straight into it. We had to walk on a narrow patch of less than two feet, to cross it. We felt the rush of water under our feet as we crossed.

Finally, things eased up a bit. Kalu turned around and smiled. We relaxed. To make things better, we met a small group of locals coming across from the other side, and then a couple more. We kept asking how much further we had to go and always got, 'Just a bit more', the standard Himalayan reply. It seemed unending, but after walking 5 km further, we finally saw a lone bulldozer fighting its way across. He had been working since morning and had cleared a patch of only 100 metres or so. The worst seemed to be over though, and we rushed onwards on the clear road. Finally, around 6.30 p.m., after walking for 30 km over twelve hours, we reached Attargu. And in a truly 'fortune favours the brave' turn of events, we saw a car standing ahead.

'Let's hope he gives us a ride till Kaza,' I spoke for everyone. We had not even thought about 'what after Attargu', we had just been so focused on getting here. The nearest village was another two hours' walk and this car was our only hope. As we approached the car, the driver got down, looked at us, and with a big smile on his face, asked, 'Mumbai?'

P.S.: The driver had been coming to this spot every morning for the last two days and had been waiting till evening. He hadn't wanted us to reach there and not find him. What would we city people think about the Spitians then?

We were speechless. We just got into the car and listened to Kalu and Lobzang talking and laughing with the driver. The drive to Kaza felt like we were floating over the road (like all drives feel after a week of walking). Kalu made a few calls to inform the local coordinators that we were on our way. By the time we reached Kaza, the news had spread.

'Are you the Mumbai couple who walked 30 km?' was the question we were asked numerous times over the next week, as we went to some of the highest villages in the world, stayed with the locals, ate some amazing food and just revelled in the general goodness of people and the slow march of time. We lived Spiti.

THE GUIDE

Spiti is the new Ladakh, and with this development, has lost some of its charm and innocence. But by any parameter, it still counts as one of the most amazing places in the world and can be truly enjoyed with a well-planned, mindful trip. Traditionally, there have been four ways to enter or exit Spiti—trek from Kinnaur and trek from Kullu (preferred ways) or by road from Lahaul over the Kunzum La Pass, and from Shimla on the Hindustan-Tibet Road along the Sutlej (long and treacherous). The trek from Kinnaur (Pin Bhabha Pass trek) continues to be the most beautiful and geographically correct way to reach Spiti. If you can, trek into Spiti—there is always the road out which you can take.

ITINERARY 6:
PIN BHABHA PASS TREK AND EXPLORING SPITI

Category: A trek combined with a road trip.

Recommended for: Those conscious of doing things the right way.

Who can do this: Those with a bit of prior trek experience, good fitness levels.

How long: 12 days.

When: July to September.

- Day 1: Reach Chandigarh (by flight / train) and drive to Fagu (or anywhere near Shimla).
- Day 2: Drive to Kinnaur and reach Sarahan, high above the Sutlej River.
- Day 3: Spend a day acclimatising in Sarahan, visit the magnificent Bhimkali temple.
- Days 4–7: Trek starts from Kafnu (two-hour drive), and over four days, takes you gradually from the million shades of green in Kinnaur to the million shades of brown in Spiti.
- Day 7: Trek ends in Mudh, in the Pin Valley of Spiti. You can spend the night here.
- Days 8 and 9: Spend two days staying with the locals in their homes. There are homestays in almost all villages of Spiti. Visit Tabo, but avoid staying in Kaza.

- Day 10: The road trip starts. Drive to Chandertal and camp there. One of the most beautiful high altitude lakes.
- Day 11: Drive across Rohtang Pass and reach Manali.
- Day 12: Either fly out of Kullu or drive to Chandigarh to take the flight or train out.

Don't miss—Homestays in Spiti

Demul, Langza and Komic are not just amongst the highest villages in the world, they also give you an opportunity to stay with the locals. Just make sure you don't insist on treating it like a hotel / guesthouse. Blend in, don't stand out.

LOCAL CONTACTS

Spiti Ecosphere is an NGO based in Kaza and is involved in all aspects of tourism in Spiti, including treks, homestays and road trips. Contact http://www.spitiecosphere.com/

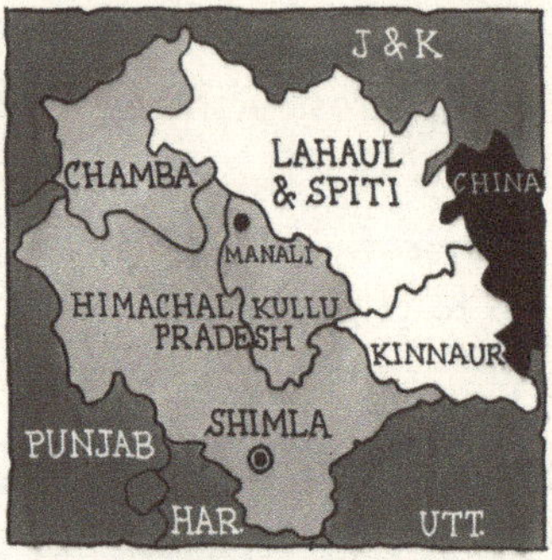

Hand-drawn maps for representation purposes only.
Not to scale.

KUGTI

The land of moonlit snows

Once you cross the Dhauladhar range around Dalhousie, you enter the middle Himalayan kingdom of Chamba. Sixty-four km north of Chamba, after a nerve-racking drive through a narrow, inhospitable gorge on a road cut through vertical rock faces, the valley opens and presents the best that the middle Himalaya has to offer: beautiful meadows, forests and fertile land. This is the town of Bharmour—the ancient capital of Chamba—under the shadow of the Mani Mahesh Peak, one of the mythical homes of Shiva. The whole land reverberates with Shiva mythology and is also known as Shiv Bhoomi. In the centre of the town is the 1,400-year-old Chaurasi temple complex, with its eighty-four shrines dedicated to Shiva. The town buzzes with pilgrims who start their Mani Mahesh pilgrimage from here between July and August.

THE MANY HOMES OF SHIVA

How many Kailashes are there? There are four famous ones. THE Kailash in Tibet, Kinner Kailash in Kinnaur, Adi Kailash in Kumaon and Mani Mahesh Kailash in Chamba. As for the rest, Shiva doesn't really have to declare every address of his. All four look remarkably similar to each other (with the exception of Kinner

Kailash) and stand out from the other mountains nearby. At least three of them have a lake at their base. So, Shiva does seem to have a preferred style. The next time you are out in the remote Himalaya, keep a look out for the local Kailash.

• • •

Bharmour is also the home to the Gaddis—the semi-nomadic shepherds who take their sheep to the pastures in and across the Pir Panjal range during summer and bring them back before winter. They are on the move for almost six months, seeking the most nutritious pastures, even if it means crossing high passes into Lahaul. One such pass is the Kugti Pass, at 5,300 metres, amongst the highest passes crossed by shepherds anywhere in the world. Every June, while the pass is still snow-bound, the Gaddis cross over and enter the Miyar Valley of Lahaul.

In June of 2014, we decided to follow in their footsteps. Once in Bharmour, our local guides informed us that, due to exceptional amounts of snow, the Gaddis hadn't yet made the first crossing of the season, although three groups of Gaddis were on their way. This necessitated an emergency visit to the Brahmani Devi temple high above the village, to seek her blessings and protection. We started the trek from the village of Kugti, and for the next three days, we trekked across forests and meadows, visited the Karthik Swamy temple overlooking the Mani Mahesh Peak and endured daily afternoon snowstorms. We met the Gaddis and their sheep every day (they were on the move too) and urged / requested them to cross the pass with us. Did they? Or were we to make our own way through thigh-deep snow? Read on.

A snow camp

'Where is the campsite?' Anjali asked. We had just finished a short climb towards the end of the third day of the trek, and reached a plateau covered entirely by snow.

'Here,' I pointed vaguely at the snow ahead.

'Here, where?' You don't want to be vague when Anjali is tired.

'Right there, on the snow, on that flat patch where the porters are sitting.' Better this time.

'We are camping on snow,' shouted an excited Amrita, before quickly taking a selfie. Those who had reached ahead of us were just sitting and staring in awe. There was more snow than any of us had seen in our lifetimes. As far as the eyes could see / miles ahead / endless … whatever description you want to apply. The high meadow, the mountains all around, everything was white. And our tryst with the snows of Kugti had begun.

The tents soon came up. Just two today, as there was only that much space and we were to sleep huddled together. That excited everyone. That, and the fact that our wake-up time was 2.30 a.m. As everyone got busy dividing themselves into two groups, I went to the guides, Pappu and Ganesh, to talk about the next day, D-day. We had passed the Gaddis and their sheep on our way to the campsite and had asked them their plans for tomorrow. They were non-committal. They don't walk with a fixed schedule in mind in any case. But it would be great for us if they did cross the pass the next day. The hundreds of sheep walking ahead would make a nice trail for us to follow on the virgin snow. We were prepared if that didn't happen, but it would be great if it did.

The guides felt that it was a 50-50 chance that the Gaddis would cross tomorrow. That's why it was important that we made our way latest by 3.30 a.m. The snow would be hard in the morning and would be perfect for walking. As the sun comes out, the snow becomes soft and is very tough to walk in. The plan was to cover as much distance as possible before it got sunny, and reach the top of the pass by 9 a.m. Going down the other side of the pass would be very tricky as the guides would have to cut steps across steep snow slopes. It would be very hard work and time-consuming.

'Yes, but it will be great if the Gaddis came too,' I said out aloud, one more time before leaving. I was obsessed with that. For months, as I was planning and visualising the trek, I hoped we would cross the pass with the Gaddis and become part of this legendary practice that has going on for centuries. And now we were almost there. And to make it even more special, this would be the first crossing of the year, something the Gaddis regard as a blessing.

The moon rises

We had dinner at 7 p.m., and it was already freezing. After a quick discussion about the next morning's plan, everyone rushed to their tents and into their sleeping bags. Good, I thought. We needed to sleep as early and as well as possible. With warmth returning to their bodies, however, everyone was soon giggling and chatting. Six in one tent, good luck with early sleep. I did my customary pee before sleeping, and just when I was getting into my tent, I could sense the sky brightening. In extreme cold, you tend to look down, close yourself, and the last thing on your mind is to take in the beauty around you. But sometimes the Himalaya forces you to look up, to appreciate the spectacular. A full moon had risen above the mountains right in front and had illuminated the entire region. The snow, below and above, was shining. It was such an amazing sight, that I had to get everyone out of their tents to see it. The cold be damned.

'Guys, you need to trust me and just come out. I know it's cold, but if you miss this, you will never forgive me. And yourself.'

It's tough not to listen to a plea like that. My trekkers emerged from their tents and looked at the moon, wide-eyed, mouths open, hearts filled.

You shouldn't miss out on this either—check the picture (does no justice to the real scene) on page v of the inserts.

Once we had our fill and the balance of cold vs awe shifted back to cold, we all went back in. Everyone was quiet, contemplating, I am sure, Nature's might, its vastness, our irrelevance and other such things that trekkers think about on nights like these. And then we went to sleep. A fitful one, like it usually is at this altitude, but we rested. As much as we needed to, I hoped, as almost everyone was awake before the first alarm rang.

'We are going to walk on snow,' Kruti said out aloud.

'Yes baby, we are!' came the reply from the next tent. And we were filled with that crazy, primordial excitement that city life had dulled, but not erased.

Excitement and cold made us finish our preparations very fast, and after a quick meal of porridge, we were ready to move. Not before the customary session of stretching though. With our headlamps on, under the moonlit sky, on shiny, hard snow, we stretched, and felt some warmth return to our bodies. I can't stress enough the importance of stretching, before and after, on easy and tough days of trekking. It makes so much difference. Anyway, we were now ready.

'Everyone, come closer,' I got into my trek leader role. 'The snow is hard, and the first stretch is almost flat, so let's cover this in quick time. This will give us time to do the final climb to the pass before the sun melts the snow.'

Even those who usually paid little attention to instructions were nodding, so I was sure the message had gotten through. It was time.

A walk on snow

We started slowly, tentatively, feeling the snow crunch under our shoes, and gradually gained confidence. We were not slipping, we were not sinking into snow, it was just like walking on a hard surface. (Check the picture on page v of the inserts.) We picked up pace. Wei Ling and Xangthe from tropical Singapore were especially in disbelief at the staggering amount of snow around them, particularly in contrast to their previous treks in parts of

Africa. It was dark, with a faint glow of the moon reflecting from the snow. Our headlamps lit the path before us. The dark forced us to focus just on the trail ahead. Walking in single file, with our individual circles of light guiding us, we must have presented a rather amusing scene for the Himalayan giants surrounding us. Insignificant dots on this massive playground. In our minds, though, we were the bravest, coolest adventurers who could do anything. Such is the duality of a Himalayan trek.

HIMALAYAN TREK CLASSIFICATION

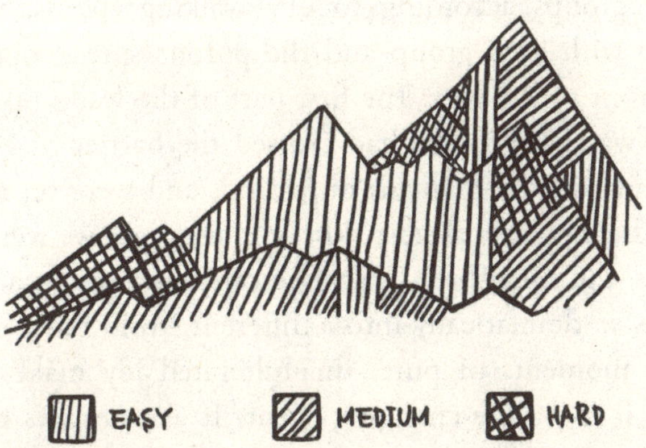

Our classification of treks into easy, medium and tough is nothing but delusions that we impose on ourselves and everyone around us. For the Himalaya, it's just another appeal for their benevolence. It usually is kind, but when it's not, trek grades do not matter. The weather doesn't go bad based on the grade of the trek and storms don't lose their intensity just because the trek is rated easy. Not just the elements, but the trail itself doesn't follow any grading. When landslides render a straight portion of the trail useless, the makeshift option is always much tougher. If the water levels in a stream increase more than is expected, crossing it becomes a nightmare. So, what is the point I am trying to make? That when in Himalaya, be grateful, be prepared and be good. The mountains are watching.

• • •

We were walking with a kind of exhilaration none of us had ever felt before. Automatically, we got divided into three groups according to our walking speeds, with a guide with each group and the porters spread out from the front to the end. The first part of the walk, up to the pass, was flattish. We had crossed the barrier of walking on snow in the night in our mind, and were on a high, in a dreamy state almost. Just five days ago, we were back home, the usual life. What else can transport us and our senses so dramatically into a different world but a dream? Such moments of pure, unadulterated joy make a trek what it is—a life-changing event. It also teaches us that nothing lasts forever.

Soon enough, the incline became steeper, breathing became laboured, thoughts were focused on just the next step, and the surreal landscape receded into the background. It was back to the grind. The pass loomed far and high off, seemingly impossible. Spirits started sagging and the guides had to prod and cheer us with 'Ho jayega'. It was too early to ask the customary question—'Aur kitna hai?' But we felt like asking. Breaks became more frequent. We became more fidgety. Removing the woollen cap, then putting it back on. Sipping on water every five minutes. Looking for excuses to stop as often as we could. Pretending to click pictures when all we wanted to do was catch our breath. And we were not even one-third of the way up. It was going to be a long day.

Two more hours passed and almost all of us managed to reach the base of the big climb to the pass, from where it gets really steep. We were short on water, tired, feeling cold and warm alternately, basically mentally fatigued. And the real tough climb was staring at us in the face. Pappu decided that this was the time for a meal break, banking on the feel-good emotion that a full stomach invariably brings. The last group—Donna and Amrita, along with Ganesh—had also caught up with us by then. We sat in a circle on the snow and opened our bags. This was not lunch, so out came the snacks. Dry fruits, dates, chikki and peanuts were shared around. Laughter made its way in, slowly but steadily. Blood sugars stabilised. Moods lifted. But then someone said, 'The snow is gonna get soft and difficult to walk in now.' And everyone started looking towards the pass with melancholy expressions.

'Yes, and a very steep incline,' I slipped that one in too. 'But remember, it's all downhill from the top.' I got some sniggers in return.

And here they come

As if burdened by the weight of Atlas, we slowly got up, brushed our behinds, slung our small day bags (the big ones were carried by porters) as if they contained rocks, and started walking in resignation. It felt like a sad scene from a Hindi movie, where the mother is hoping against hope that her son will come. And just like he usually does, our heroes chose that moment to make their entry.

First we heard just the whistle. For the last three days, we had been walking with and around the Gaddis and we were all familiar with this peculiar sound. With wet eyes and expectation on our faces, we all looked back and waited. The first sheep appeared after five minutes, and soon enough, they were all there. Three groups of Gaddis with four hundred sheep each. The shouts of 'Har har Mahadev' booming in the air. They had decided to cross the pass today after all. Picture on page vi of the inserts.

I was delirious with joy and might have shouted things like '… the trek is all but done', etc. The 1,200 sheep would walk ahead of us and make a path for us up the pass and then down to the other side. All we had to do was follow their footsteps. Simple. Aarti, who was walking next to me, had no option but to share my excitement.

'Why am I so happy seeing the Gaddis, remind me please?' she asked, after high-fiving me. I gathered everyone around me and explained my theory. I then asked them to wait and let the sheep go ahead. Within a few minutes, the Gaddis were with us, seeming equally happy to see us as we were to see them.

'Humko aap ka support milega,' one of them said. Oh, who was supporting whom?

'They are just being modest,' I said out aloud, really hoping that was the case.

Step 1 didn't go as per the plan. The 1,200 sheep didn't walk up the slope in one line. They spread out and almost ran up, in the process softening the snow. Exactly what we didn't want.

'What are you waiting for, no one is coming to rescue you,' Pappu mock-shouted at us. So we started plodding up. We soon figured out that the sheep hoofprints were keeping us from slipping down as we climbed up. So maybe they did help us after all. Whatever the case, we had no bandwidth to think. Our hearts were pounding so loudly, that it shut us off from everything else. Every step was a huge effort. You can join us in spirit—picture on page vi of the inserts.

We were now sinking knee-deep with every step, and sometimes thigh-deep too, depending on where we chose to place our feet. The Gaddis, who were expecting support from us, were almost at the top of the pass with their sheep. Aarti was convinced that they knew of a shortcut and insisted that we look for it rather than climb up this way, and took off in some random direction. She had to be literally dragged back.

Beyond fatigue, there is a stage of delirium. I thought that's where most of us were as we walked up that slope that day. Loudly panting, groaning, then laughing and shouting for no reason. Thankfully, this lasted for a very short while and was rudely broken when we saw a trail of red coming down all the way from the top. This was, we later found out, the customary offering to the Goddess who resides at the top of this mountain and allows the Gaddis to pass. In every first crossing of the season, a sheep is sacrificed. It had the effect of sobering us and we focused back on the trail with our limited mind spaces.

The closer we got to the top, the tougher it became. It always does. In your mind, you have already reached, but physically there are these last few steps. After each step, you look up, lungs screaming, and you so desperately are hoping it's the last. But there is no option but to take the next step, and the next, the karma of a trekker. And finally, once this lesson is learnt, you reach the top.

At the top

If you have ever wondered what it is like at the top of the high mountains you see from the hill stations, let me tell you. There is cold. That's the first thing. Then there is the wind, which only makes it colder. And there is snow and rock all around you, all encompassing. But, and this is an important 'but', there is also a feeling of exhilaration, a much profounder version of butterflies in the stomach before a date, or unexpectedly winning the school 100-metres race. There is a sense of achievement, usually followed by tears of joy and relief. And finally there is euphoria. Your trek-mates, people you have met for the first time just a few days ago, and with whom you are now sharing this moment, become etched in your heart forever. The best friendships are made on the top of a pass on a Himalayan trek. And once your heart rate slows down a bit and the initial euphoria passes, your eyes take over. Through them you see the sights no one can describe. You know that you are now a part of the mountains and they are a part of you.

There is also hunger, thirst, fear, apprehension, headache and more. But who wants to know about that, right? In our case, there was something else, much more intense, much more dangerous—the wait. The first two groups had reached the top by 9.30 a.m. And they had to share the small space at the top with 1,200 sheep. The Gaddis were performing an elaborate ritual (which also included the sacrifice) that was taking a lot of time. On the other side of the pass, the slope was so steep that it was impossible for even the sheep to walk down. The Gaddis would have to make a path for them for about 100 metres, which would traverse the steepest section of the slope. Once the sheep crossed that section, they would be able to go down on their own. We would then walk the same path. But for that to happen, we had to first wait.

This was the scene—at the top of the pass, at 5,300 metres, sitting on a small rocky outcrop with snow all around, were us and our porters and guides. A little to the side were the three Gaddis doing their offerings. From the Kugti side, the last members of our group were coming up, extremely slowly. On the Lahaul side, 1,200 sheep were packed together waiting to go down. On either side, the nearest village was at least a two-day walk away. There was no water source for us to refill our bottles. And the Gaddis wouldn't allow us to pee, as this was a sacred place. It was worse for our porters. Not only were they carrying all the baggage, they were observing a strict fast as is customary when crossing the Kugti Pass. No food and no water.

Let's distract ourselves now by checking on the last

group. About a hundred steps below the pass, Amrita was slowly inching upwards, followed by a completely dazed Xangthe. A few steps behind them was Donna, twice the size of Ganesh, almost being carried by Ganesh. He was physically lifting one leg of hers, then the other, placing them in front, making her walk. And while he was almost dying from the effort, Donna was instructing him 'ache se rakho, thoda aage'. And then, Donna sat. Ganesh waited patiently. After five minutes passed, he prodded her to get up. Donna kept sitting. She couldn't get up, she said. Ganesh tried his best to pull her and push her, but Donna couldn't move. The situation called for additional deployment of forces. Down went Pappu and Lucky (the girl's favourite porter). But all three couldn't move her. Let me take a moment to inform you that this is a true story. Okay, so the guides and porters figured that it's not about force—they needed a strategy. A rope was called for. It was tied around her waist. Lucky then tied the other end around his waist and stood in front. Pappu pulled on the rope and Ganesh pushed Donna. And finally Donna moved.

'Don't stop till you reach the top now,' we all shouted.

The school of snowball throwing

Once Donna, Amrita and Xangthe reached the top and settled down, we had no further interest in this side of the mountain. And so we all turned to see what was happening with the sheep and the Gaddis. The three Gaddis along with Pappu and his beloved ice axe, had made a small path horizontally across the slope for the sheep. But the problem was, no matter how much they tried, the sheep were not moving ahead. The reason, we learnt soon, was that the first sheep who had tried to, slipped and fell to her death all the way down the mountain.

'They have four legs, we have two, how the hell are we going to walk across?' Usha put in words what all of us were thinking. But there was a lot happening and our thoughts didn't linger long enough.

The Gaddis were pushing the sheep forward, urging them to move, only to be pushed back. All this time, they were standing on the narrow ledge, from where when someone falls, they die. The brave sheep in front, which were no longer so brave, had blocked the narrow path and there was no way anyone could reach them. Do check the picture on page vii of the inserts. Then started a snowball throwing competition, wherein the Gaddis tried to prod the sheep forward by throwing snowballs at them. The hit rate was one in fifty maybe. Most of the time, the snowballs flew ahead or hit the sheep in the back, the ones that could anyway not move forward. And even when the snowball hit the sheep in front, all she did was move two steps and then again stop. Once in a while, the very first sheep would just turn around and push her way back. Everyone would follow her and the wave would reach all the way till the end of the line, where the Gaddis would once again push them back. Like a perfect spring.

It was the ultimate test of patience, especially at that altitude, for us thirsty and bladder-full trekkers. With nothing better to do, our guides and porters also joined the game. Not that they were any better. I proposed a new academy in Kugti village for Gaddis, where they would be taught to throw more accurately. It was a life-saving skill after all.

'Don't just sit, help,' Pappu shouted at us. Like clockwork, he would shout once every hour. And so the twelve of us were also throwing snowballs now. By sheer increase in the volume, the sheep in front were getting hit more often, and they were reluctantly moving ahead. Progress was being made, every inch counted and cheered. And finally, the first sheep crossed the dangerous 100 metres mark and was on safe ground. She looked bewildered for a moment before rushing down the less steep slope. Predictably, the rest followed, and within minutes the logjam cleared, giving way to smooth-flowing traffic. Even better, while going down, they all followed one path and made a nice way for us. I gave Anjali a triumphant look.

Things moved fast, the Gaddis followed their sheep and soon it was our turn to get going. It was past noon, and we had spent almost three hours at that altitude. Luckily, the weather was good, but soon it would be time for the customary afternoon snowfall. The whole snowball-throwing exercise had acted as a good warm-up for us and we were physically ready to go.

Mentally, though, it was a different game altogether. All twelve of us were now standing at the same place the sheep had been some time back, and we were hoping that our Gaddis, i.e. the guides and porters, would somehow take us across. Usha, who was lost in God-knows-what thoughts, slipped while standing and Pappu stopped her from sliding down. Everyone was shocked and became even more psyched.

'If I had fallen down, what would have happened?' Usha asked Pappu rhetorically.

'Direct to Mahadev,' Pappu looked towards the sky and replied with a deadpan expression.

'I have two young kids back home, I don't want to die, Rujuta.'

'You hold my hand, and don't leave it,' Rujuta consoled her.

An accident on the slopes of Kugti Pass

Note: From here on, we separated into two groups, so the narrative will move back and forth, please bear with me.

Without thinking much, the six of us who were ahead in the queue, along with three porters, started the walk. 'Lean on the mountain side'—the familiar instruction was never so seriously followed. We leaned on the slope to our left, our hands trying for some grip in the snow and our feet barely fitting on the path. One step at a time, we moved ahead. The dead sheep at the bottom of the slope on the right was a constant reminder to us not to lose focus. Every time we slipped, the porters would shout at us, as it damaged the narrow path to salvation and they had to mend it for those who came behind. Time stood absolutely still and the only measurement was the number of steps. The porters with us were young boys who didn't know fear, and some of their attitude rubbed off on us. And in about twenty minutes, we were through, hugging and high-fiving each other. Not for a moment did we think about those yet to cross—it was the joy of surviving.

The 'fearless' streak continued when the porters suggested that we slide down the narrow, one-foot deep path the sheep had made for us. One by one we sat down on the path with our ponchos under our bums. With basic instructions from the porters about using our heels and elbows as brakes and steering, we slid down at high speed. The path wound around the slope and we were like a solo luge, but without a sled. The reason it was safe was because the path was narrow and deep, and we could fit inside it, so there was no chance of falling off. Of course, it was full of sheep poo and yellow piss, but that we ignored as we zoomed down. It was super fast and in less than two minutes we came down almost 1.5 km, and stopped when the slope became flat. For a moment, imagine the most thrilling ride of your life. In a theme park or (hopefully not) in a very fast car. Multiply it by ten. That was the feeling we had, as the adrenaline rush was overwhelming.

'Paisa vasool,' was the first thing Guptaji said after touchdown. It truly was. A picture of the slope we slid down is on page vii of the inserts.

Group 2 barely noticed us sliding down and the fun we were having. It was the first stretch that mattered. They had Pappu and Ganesh, along with Lucky and a few other porters, to take them across. Holding hands, silently praying, listening to Pappu's warnings, they managed to cross the difficult part. Pappu was on a high and he insisted that everyone slide straight down the slope by making a train, and not on the narrow path that the first group had taken.

If Pappu was saying so, why not, thought everyone. In the front sat Pappu, behind him was Aarti with her legs locked around Pappu, and then came Usha with her legs around Aarti, and in the end Rujuta, true to her word, holding on firmly to Usha's backpack. Three such trains were formed, the second piloted by Ganesh and the third by Lucky. Apparently, there was a scramble to sit behind Lucky but no one admitted to that later.

Anyway, the first train started the ride down with Pappu controlling it with his ice axe and feet. Everyone behind him was screaming. It was all fun and laughter, until the point when Pappu's ice axe slipped from his hand and fell to the side. That ice axe was like his third hand. Pappu forgot where he was and what he was doing. He just instinctively swerved sharply to his right, trying to grab the ice axe. The high speed train was suddenly without the engine and the three bogeys derailed spectacularly. Rujuta held on to Usha while trying hard to brake with her shoes, but the momentum carried them downwards. Finally, and sensibly, she let go of Usha's backpack. Both slowed down and stopped shortly after that. Aarti, on the other hand, was on a roll, literally. She took a 180-degree turn and was on her stomach, her head facing downhill. For more than thirty seconds, which surely must have felt much, much longer, she hurtled down the slope screaming loudly, somehow avoiding the small rocks on the way, before finally rolling on her back again and coming to a stop. Then she lay quiet and still.

Ganesh, who was leading the second train, applied 'emergency brakes', and ensured that everyone behind him was fine. Then, he ran / slid down to Aarti in record time.

'Aarti madam, aankhen kholo please,' he pleaded, gently slapping her face.

'Main zinda hoon, Ganesh,' Aarti madam said. Ganesh laughed and the spell that everyone was under was broken. Soon everyone made their way to Aarti and she showed them the burn marks on her stomach due to all the sliding. Aarti presented a brave front, but it obviously hurt a lot. Pappu reached the spot too, sheepishly caressing his ice axe and saying something which sounded like an apology.

'I think we should walk down the slope now, slowly,' he said.

'That's a good idea, Pappu,' Anjali replied.

The afternoon storm

Meanwhile, we in the first group were having a great time. We were on a high after sliding down. There was also the knowledge that the difficult part of the day was over. It was a matter of just following the trail now. Conveniently, the cook and his team who had gone ahead with the Gaddis had left their footprints on the snow. All we had to do was follow these, to reach the campsite. However, we were very thirsty. One of the porters spotted a small waterfall some distance away and we decided to head there to fill water. We drank water, ate whatever was left in our bags, looked back at the slope where we could make out some dots in the middle of the slope, shrugged and started walking. And just then, without any warning, clouds moved in. At that altitude, when clouds move in, you are inside the clouds. Everything around us turned white and it started snowing. We didn't know whether to be thrilled or scared, so we decided to be thrilled. The footprints were still visible after all.

We followed the trail like purebred bloodhounds. Even when it entered a jumble of streams and a marshy area, going up and down small snow hills, we trusted it. The three porters were leading us and they obviously knew where they were going. Until, one of them turned around and announced, 'We don't know where we are going. It is our first time here, we are just following the footprints, but this doesn't seem like the right path,' he said in Hindi. Wow. Getting lost in the whiteout was the only thing left for us to experience. The cooks obviously had taken this path, so even if this was not *the* right trail, it was still *a* trail that would lead us to the campsite, was the consensus. At such times, hope works wonders. We continued on the trail. The problem was, the footprints were disappearing under fresh snow.

About half an hour later, when the footprints were barely visible, the snowfall stopped. 'Inscrutable are your favours, O Lord'—I remembered this dialogue from some random movie I had seen. The whiteout also started clearing and we could make out that we were walking on a ridge. Below, to our right, was a wide, flat patch which appeared to me like the correct path. I was by then in 'trip leader' mode again and felt it was up to me to lead my group to safety.

'I think we have to go down there. Follow me.' And without looking back I started walking down, scrambling in knee deep snow. Midway, when I realised that this was not a good idea, I looked back to call off the plan, only to find that no one had followed me and had instead carried on with the porters.

'They chose well,' I consoled myself. For me, though, the choice was made as climbing back up was much more difficult than coming down. Stumbling and tumbling, with my ego slightly bruised, I managed to come down the slope and get on the flat patch. And lo and behold, there was a figure in the distance coming towards me.

Usha appeared out of the whiteout like a ghost. She was totally confused as to why I was so excited to see her and was hugging her. I tried telling her how I had 'bravely' come down the slope and no one had followed me, etc., etc., but she was least interested.

'How much more before this day gets over?' was her only query.

'Ahem, just an hour more,' I replied, without any idea. She continued walking silently. I followed her for some time till I heard a voice from behind. I stopped and waited. It was Rujuta. Never had I felt so good seeing another human being. She was just the person I needed. She was in control, strong; she gave me a hug, told me that all was okay with the others behind her and that everyone had done well. She even indulged me by listening to my story of 'bravery'. I actually teared up a little.

The update from her was that those who had been doing well in the first half of the day were now tired and zoned out (and bruised in Aarti's case). On the other hand, those who had really struggled, like Xangthe, Amrita and especially Donna, were finding the way down much easier and were doing great.

'Everyone had a complete experience,' I joked and we started walking down. But I was constantly looking up towards the ridge, hoping to spot someone from the first group. Finally, I told Rujuta that I had to go and look for them. With a heavy heart I turned around, and even entertained some thoughts about my commitment. But in just about fifteen minutes, I saw the first group climbing down the ridge much ahead of where I was and closer to our campsite. They had really chosen well.

The longest day of our lives

If you have stuck around with me till here, you are a patient person, but I must hurry and wrap up this account. Down the slope, where the snow was less, was the trekker's hut. Usually, the sight of the campsite at the end of a trek day elicits joy and excitement from tired bodies. But today was anything but usual. When I reached the hut, it was silent, with those inside lying on their backs with their legs up against the wall. Further inside, in the small adjoining room, the cooks and porters had set up the kitchen. These guys had not eaten or drunk anything all day, had carried our loads and were obviously tired. But they were still doing what they had to, and with a smile. A fire was up and running, hot soup was in the works.

This was the pattern—a trekker would reach the hut, remove his / her shoes and socks, throw them away actually, contemplate complaining and screaming but instead accept the mug of hot soup from the porters and drain it, all the while staring in amusement at all the others in Vipareeta Karni, before joining them quietly after a while. The first words would be uttered only after five minutes in that position, and that would mostly be '... what a day'. Time tempers your feelings like nothing else. Time and a warm hut. By 6.30 p.m., everyone was inside the hut, safe, snug and hungry. We had spent the last twenty-four hours in snow, and most of us had had our fill of it for years to come, if not lifetimes. It was all over us, from inside our socks to our underclothes. But we were beyond caring.

The porters had left all the 'non-essential' stuff back at the previous campsite (from where it would be taken back to Kugti village by another support team), and that included the kerosene canister, the stove and most vegetables. Every ounce mattered for them and they did the best they could. So it was wood fire-cooked khichdi for us that night. The wet wood generated more smoke than heat though, and our impatience was growing by the minute. I tried to distract everyone by getting them to change into new sets of clothes and setting up our sleeping bags for the night. When there was nothing else left to do, the group crowded around the kitchen and literally forced the cook to bring the khichdi out. We gulped down the half-cooked khichdi, at the cost of upsetting the cook, and were still hungry. Whatever little snacks were left were also devoured. And then, finally, the mountains decided to bless us.

Leh, the heart of Ladakh

The village of Rumbak, home of the snow leopard

Pangong Tso, beyond words

Steep descent all the way to Kali

The meadows of Chialekh

The sinking village of Garbyal

The first view of Kuthi village

The first view of Adi Kailash from the pasture

The legendary rice fields of Jolingkong

The pink river, Pin valley, Spiti

Mudh village, and the stream that was flooded is on the left

The moon rises above our campsite

Pre-dawn walk on hard, crisp snow

Here come the Gaddis and their sheep

The final steep climb to Kugti Pass

The bottleneck at the top of Kugti Pass, towards the Lahaul side

The steep slope after Kugti Pass; the treacherous 100 metres is marked in red, and the subsequent path that we slid on is marked green

Ghamsali, the second-last village before Tibet

A glimpse of Nanda Devi from Auli

A bright morning at the campsite ahead of Ghamsali

The women of Lata discussing the selling price of their carpets

Lunch before the afternoon drizzle

The Damarsain meadows

The trail through dense vegetation

The trail to Khan Pari Pass

A well-deserved rest at the top

Coming down in a whiteout

An open-air breakfast

The Gaddi's sheep in the surreal meadows of Khan Pari

Rujuta and the Gaddi

A lookout

Uday, the Gaddi

With the women of Shankchar

The rainbow on Kinner Kailash, from Kalpa

The gathering of gods in Kalpa

The moon rises over the Kinner Kailash range

Landslide before Sangla

The fields of Ogra in Sangla valley

The Kamru fort

Sheep take a reluctant bath

The trail to Nagasthi; Sangla river on the right

The valley opens up just before Thangu

The Chopta valley – what lies ahead?

The masked dance at Thangu monastery

Gurudongmar lake, and the glacier that feeds it

Rujuta was trying to look for some woollens in her backpack when she found a packet of her special puran poli. She had carried it with her from Mumbai, and had completely forgotten about it. The puran poli were crushed into small bits, but that didn't matter. Not just that, she was carrying desi ghee, which she does on all treks. We heated the ghee, poured it on the crushed puran polis and ate them slowly, relishing them, sharing them around with the porters and guides, understanding that the mountains had truly looked after us. We were then full and satisfied, and slept a healing sleep in a small hut in the middle of the high Himalaya.

P.S.: The next day dawned nice and bright. We woke up with no memory of the aches and pains of the previous day and were in high spirits. There was tonnes of laughter, and a photo session ensued. Selfies, group pictures, pictures with Pappu and all the other guides and porters, and many, many pictures with Lucky. It was the last day of the trek, and after the initial scramble down a slope, we walked along a small canal all the way to the first village in Lahaul. The villagers were working in their beautiful potato fields and we chatted with them, showing off our accomplishment of the first crossing of the Kugti Pass this season. We didn't meet the Gaddis despite our so wanting to, as they had gone ahead already. By 1 p.m. we reached the roadhead, had a surprisingly amazing lunch at a roadside dhaba (or maybe we were just very hungry), drove to Udaipur to see the wooden carvings at the legendary Mrikula Devi temple (if you are ever in Lahaul, DO NOT miss it) and finally reached our guesthouse in the evening, to a hot water bath and a bed, the ultimate luxuries of life. It's been four years since the trek, but everyone still wishes each other on the anniversary of the day we crossed the Kugti Pass.

THE GUIDE

Chamba and Lahaul are perhaps the least-visited regions of a very tourist-friendly Himachal. They retain their rawness, that wild nature of the high mountains and remote valleys. Lack of access roads was one of the main reasons for its seclusion, but that is changing now. Here are some ways you can explore this region.

ITINERARY 7: THE VALLEYS OF PANGI AND LAHAUL

Category: A road trip through extremely remote valleys.

Recommended for: Those looking to go beyond the normal.

Who can do this: Anyone with an appetite for risk and a flexible schedule.

How long: 7 days.

When: July to September

- Day 1: Reach Amritsar by flight or train. Drive to Dalhousie. (You can also fly into Dharamshala.) Dalhousie is one of the top five hill stations of India, so expect lots of crowds during summer vacation.
- Day 2: Drive to Pangi, via the Sach Pass, a thrilling drive on one of the newest routes in the Himalaya (for cars, otherwise a very old trek route). Stay in Killar and make it the base for exploring the sub-valleys of Pangi. Basic accommodation available.
- Day 3: Drive to Sural Valley and reach the last village, Sural Bhatori. Walk around the village and see the monastery. Return to Killar.
- Day 4: Drive to Hudan Valley and reach the last village, Hudan Bhatori. Do a short walk ahead of

the village to a small pond and the grazing ground. Excellent views from there. Return to Killar.

- Day 5: Drive to Miyar Valley and stay the night in Urgus village, in a homestay. It's one of the prettiest villages you will ever see and makes for a perfect walk around.
- Day 6: Early morning, leave from Urgus, cross Rohtang Pass and reach Manali. Stay in Naggar to avoid the crowds after so many days in the relative wilderness.
- Day 7: Fly out or drive to Chandigarh.

ITINERARY 8: THE MIYAR VALLEY TREK

Category: Easy trek in Miyar Valley.

Recommended for: First-time trekkers who want the thrill of the unknown.

Who can do this: Everyone with basic fitness levels.

How long: 7 days.

When: June to September.

- Day 1 and 2: Reach Urgos either via Chamba and Pangi valley (Itinerary 7) or via Manali, Rohtang Pass.

- Day 3-5: Easy walks in Miyar Valley, with some beautiful campsites and accessible glaciers.
- Day 5: Finish the trek and come back to Udaipur or Keylong.
- Days 6 and 7: Same as Itinerary 7.

Here comes my Bollywood connection—In June 2010, ten of us went for the Miyar Valley trek. With us was a shy teenager who had come along with her mother and aunt. While walking on the trail above Urgos, the tired girl wanted to take a quick break and sat on a stone by the edge of the road. The stone was unstable and as soon as she sat down, it wobbled and almost rolled down the slope. Alia Bhat was quick to get up and move on. And just when she finished the trek, she got a call for *Student of the Year.*

ITINERARY 9: TREK FROM CHAMBA TO LAHAUL

Category: Trek across the Pir Panjal range.

Recommended for: Trekkers who don't like crowded trails.

Who can do this: Good fitness levels and / or prior trek experience.

How long: 9 days.

When: June to September.

- Day 1: Reach Amritsar by flight or train. Drive to Dalhousie or Chamba.
- Day 2: Drive to and reach Bharmour.
- Day 3: Drive + walk to the village of Kugti and stay the night there.
- Days 4–7: Trek across the Kugti Pass over the next four days and reach Lahaul.
- Day 7: Reach the road and drive to Keylong for the night.
- Day 8: Leave early and cross Rohtang Pass to enter Manali. Spend the night there or in Naggar, just 15 km ahead.
- Day 9: Fly out or drive to Chandigarh.

ITINERARY 9A: MANI MAHESH PARIKRAMA

- Days 1–2: Same as Itinerary 8.
- Days 3–5: Do the legendary parikrama of the Mani Mahesh (specific time of the year only).
- Day 5: Finish the trek and back to Bharmour.
- Day 6: Drive back to Chamba.
- Day 7: Drive to Amritsar or Dharamshala for the flight back.

LOCAL CONTACTS

1. We trekked with Anna Adventures. Don't get confused with the name. It's not the south Indian 'Anna', but is the English Anna, the name of the daughter of the local guide who runs this agency. Contact http://bharmourtreks.com/
2. Urgos Homestay. Contact Sadev Singh on 9459989133.

Hand-drawn maps for representation purposes only.
Not to scale.

DAMARSAIN MEADOWS

And the second-last village in India

Badrinath is the most popular amongst the extremely popular Char Dhams in Garhwal. Thousands of visitors / pilgrims drive to Badrinath (or take a helicopter ride) every week during the season. In May and June especially, there are hours-long traffic jams and every available hotel / guesthouse is packed. The pilgrims are on a strict schedule. They usually come to Badrinath after visiting the other three Dhams and are now towards the end of their crazy road journey. They are exhausted, to say the least, and have no time or inclination to explore. From their base in Joshimath, they make a day's trip to Badrinath and back. Very few, if any, consider the option of a day trip to Auli, beautiful meadows reachable by road with some of the best views in the Himalaya. Even fewer venture into the Niti Valley and visit the historic villages of Lata and Reni, right on the edge of the Nanda Devi Sanctuary. No one goes beyond Lata. This is an account of our trip in October 2014 beyond Lata, to Ghamsali, the second-last village before Tibet, and to Damarsain meadows, a short, easy trek away.

Ghamsali

Long after we had been stunned into silence by the sheer scale of the Himalaya, by the remoteness of the valley we were passing through, by the roaring waters of the Dhauli Ganga and by the gradual transition of evening to dusk, our cars took one final turn and stopped in front of the second-last village in India. In slow motion we got out, our mouths half-open, eyes popping, darting alternately to the glaciers running down the high mountains on our left and right, and at Ghamsali in front of us, a village unlike any we had ever seen. We had long given up on any notions of 'normal'. The Greater Himalayan range lies beyond normal, but Ghamsali was challenging our concepts of 'spectacular', 'extraordinary', and such. What had till now appeared as random boulders strewn across a flattish land were actually strategic wind-breakers, and nestled, and I mean literally nestled, under and amidst them, were the homes. It had rained recently, and the spent clouds were now drifting aimlessly between the folds of the mountains. It was October and the meadows around the village were golden in colour. We had just stepped out of our cars and into a postcard. See picture on page viii of the inserts.

Our guide, Sunil, who had maintained his poise throughout the day while answering with a 'You will see why' to our repeated question as to '... why the second-last village, who goes to the second-last one, why not to Niti, the last village', had an 'I told you so' smile on his face. We started to slowly walk towards the village. The path was spotlessly clean, the houses were beautiful, made of stone, with slate roofs and intricate woodwork on the windows. Wait, woodwork? There were hardly any trees around. We were above the tree line and this was deodar wood, royalty amongst all Himalayan trees.

'How about a short lesson in history?'

Sunil was waiting for this moment. This is what he told us.

For centuries, Niti Valley, that is the name of the valley we had travelled through today from Joshimath onwards for more than six hours, was a legendary trade route to Tibet. Inhabited by the Bhotiya tribe, a group of people of Mongoloid origin who follow Hinduism and Tibetan Buddhism, the villages in this valley had grown prosperous from the trade of wool, salt, etc. And we could vouch that they had a taste for the good things. Deodar wood was procured from down the valley and expert artisans were summoned from far off places. The intricacy of the woodwork was on par with the best of work done in temples and palaces in the lower hills. They had limited contact with what they now know as India, and their trade with Tibet was their identity. And then suddenly, out of the blue, the country they didn't even know existed, demanded or rather enforced a complete ban on the trade with Tibet (after the 1962 war). An entire way of life altered overnight. Generations of traders were now herders and grazers, and only their pride in their history keeps them here.

The Bhotiyas of Niti Valley practice transhumance, wherein the entire population moves from the villages to a lower altitude during winter, and then back again to the villages and high altitude meadows with their cattle during summer. The Ghamsali villagers were the envy of the entire Niti Valley, for they had access to the best of meadows, with the most nutritious grass, and for a trekker, the most amazing views. These were the meadows of Damarsain, at 3,600 metres above sea level, a wide open pastureland full of flowers in summer and snow in winter. And this is where we were heading the next day.

But before that, we had to pitch camp for the night. Just 500 metres ahead of the village, there is flat land, Sunil told us. He lamented that his group had not yet been able to start the concept of homestays in this beautiful village, but was hoping to do so soon. We walked through the fields in almost pitch darkness, with the aid of our head lamps. The guides, porters and cooks quickly set up the tents, while we helped the best we could. The glaciers were still shining in the star light, but everything else was behind the veil of darkness. We were at 3,300 metres and the only reason none of us felt the effects of altitude, was because we had spent the last two nights in Auli, acclimatising and preparing for the trek. We had stayed at the appropriately-named Nanda Devi Lodge run by Sunil's group, with a view that has no parallel. From the first floor living room, Nanda Devi loomed right in front. Sometimes clear, sometimes behind clouds, it enthralled us for most of those two days. A picture on page viii of the inserts will give you an idea.

Now here, in Ghamsali, we were right on the edge of the outer Nanda Devi Sanctuary. So many stories, so many legends to contemplate as we dropped off to sleep.

THE NANDA DEVI

The highest Himalayan peak completely within the Indian boundary (Kangchendzonga shares a border with Nepal), Nanda Devi is much more than just a mountain. She is the Mother Goddess of Uttarakhand, and all the devis and devtas pay obeisance to her. Once every twelve years, a one-horned ram is born in one of the villages around the sanctuary and leads a remarkable pilgrimage to Nanda Devi. Hundreds of villagers climb, singing and dancing for days together, as they trek in extreme conditions, carried forward by faith and nothing else.

Nanda Devi lies in the centre of two concentric rings made up of high Himalayan peaks. It forms a biosphere of its own, probably the last such ecosystem anywhere in the world. And obviously, irresistible to humans. Explorers tried for years before Shipton and Tillman found a way to the inner sanctuary in 1935. For the next four decades, expedition after expedition went in, destroying the same ecosystem they came to 'study'. The government had to finally ban entry to the outer and inner sanctuary to preserve the ecosystem, and perhaps also to keep the secret of the nuclear device lost on its slopes (discussed below).

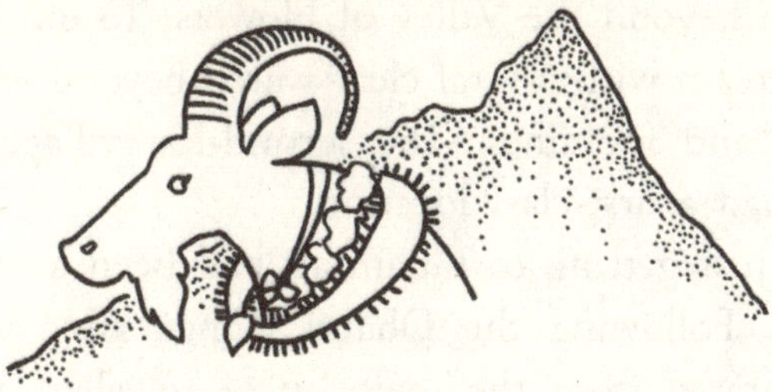

• • •

The morning welcomed us with even more fantastic scenes of the high mountains, clear blue skies, floating clouds and golden grass all around us. Check the picture on page viii of the inserts. Since this was a short two-day trek back and forth to the meadows, we were in no hurry to leave this beautiful campsite. A lazy breakfast of aloo parantha and omelette with bread and butter followed, while sitting out under the warm October sun and feasting our eyes on the view around us. Afterwards, it was time for endless cups of hot tea, and only when the cook announced that he was packing up the kitchen, did we finally get up and start to prep for the walk. Most of the Ghamsali villagers had brought their cattle back from the meadows, Sunil told us. So we would have them entirely to ourselves.

Soon we started walking. It was one of those leisurely walks, easy on the body, but overwhelming for the eyes. To our right were huge mountains, their rocky faces shining in the sun. Every time we looked at them, we couldn't get over the fact that these belong to the outer ring of the Nanda Devi Sanctuary, and that we were trekking in a region beyond the Valley of Flowers. To our left was a small stream with crystal clear water, beyond which were glaciers and moraines. The second-last village in India surely had a first-class location.

But just getting to Ghamsali had been a memorable journey. Following the Dhauli Ganga after Joshimath, we separated from the majority of travellers who were headed for Badrinath. And just like that, within a matter of minutes, we were in an untouched land which was in the process of getting officially 'connected'. The river was being subjected to some massive hydel power projects and deep gashes were visible on the mountains on both sides. As usual, the government had tried to push through multiple projects, knowing well that the locals would resist, and as a compromise they would then sanction only that many as they anyway wanted to.

Our first stop was the legendary village of Lata, the gateway to the Nanda Devi inner sanctuary, till date the only viable route inside. The cars were parked on the road and we climbed steeply up the mountain to reach the village. Totally out of breath, we were offered tea and biscuits in one of the Bhotiya homes, which was part of Sunil's organisation. The sweet tea helped. We had limited time, so Sunil moved fast. We went to the village centre, a small courtyard. Sunil shouted out loudly that visitors have come. Out came the women of Lata. Wearing their local dresses, proud, strong.

The women of Lata

Since ours was an organised trip, it followed a standard template. Visitors, the local organisation hoped, would come to these forgotten villages, meet the local people, and perhaps buy some handicrafts, etc. To that end, the women brought with them some jewellery made of semi-precious stones, some shawls and other woollens. But most of us were fascinated with the carpets of all sizes that were drying on rooftops all around. When they noticed us looking at them, the entire village brought out the carpets they had woven. A mini bazaar was set up and the carpets were displayed. Since there was no concept of selling the carpets, they had no idea what to charge. The elders were summoned and a passionate discussion ensued between them. The picture on page ix of the inserts is a must-see. My group was well-trained to not bargain with villagers, and to pay what they asked. Finally, when the prices were announced, they were much less than any of us had imagined they would be. A couple of expert shoppers in our group took Sunil aside and told him that the carpets were being undervalued and that they should charge more. A revised price was put forth and all of us bought handmade, traditionally-designed, plant-dyed carpets from a very happy bunch of Lata women.

These were not ordinary women though; they had once forced the government to bend. One of the most successful grassroots conservation movements of all time, anywhere in the world, the Chipko Movement started right here, in the villages of Lata and Reni (across the river). After the 1962 war, which deprived this entire valley of its livelihood, the Indian government built the road and basic infrastructure in the area, but the only ones to benefit seemed to be the timber mafia. As they started cutting down the forest recklessly, the locals, fresh from the wounds of the closed trade, finally put their foot down and a spark of resistance started from these villages in 1974. Here, an elderly Gaura Devi emerged as the leader of a group of women who simply clung to the trees which were about to be cut, and forced the axe-wielders out. The movement soon spread to other parts of Garhwal and Kumaon, and became the first and most successful environmentally-inspired uprising of the poor.

Damarsain meadows

Let's get back to the trek now. From Ghamsali, we walked for four hours through some of the best scenery you will ever see. The climb was very gradual, from 3,300 to 3,600 metres over 5-6 km, and the day was beautiful. We had many stops, not because we were tired, but because we could. Sunil told us many stories, we took many pictures, and generally enjoyed ourselves. Those who had trekked before were especially savouring the day, remembering all the struggles on past treks to get to similar meadows. Soon, we saw that we were on level with the stream and watched it meandering through the flat land ahead. A perfect place to graze, with abundant grass and water. The Damarsain meadows. Picture on page ix of the inserts. By 1 p.m., we were there and the first thing we did was have lunch. We were hungry, plus the clouds had started building up for their customary afternoon show. Check the picture on page ix of the inserts of our lunch at Damarsain meadows. As soon as we were done, the first drops came down and we all went inside the big dining tent. We chatted and played a few games of Mafia, before Sunil came in with hot tea and more stories—of the third act in the life of the Niti Valley Bhotiyas after the 1962 war and the 1974 Chipko Movement.

In 1982, the Nanda Devi Sanctuary, the traditional grazing ground of all the villages in the Niti Valley, and a significant contributor to the local economy (as the expeditions that arrived here to climb and explore would hire local men as guides and porters), was closed down not just for outsiders but for the natives too. Once again, all this happened overnight. It delivered a crippling blow to the already floundering economy and affected more than 80 per cent of families in the valley directly. Ostensibly, the reason for the closure of the sanctuary was to preserve the bio-diversity and the ecology that had undergone extensive damage because of unregulated expeditions. However, a far more sinister motive came to the fore a few years later, when it was discovered that the CIA and the Indian Army had indulged in some Cold

War era secret project, wherein a nuclear tracking device (to track China's movements across the border) was to be placed on top of the Nanda Devi mountain. Lost to them was the fact that the Nanda Devi was more than a mountain, it was the reigning Goddess for most of Garhwal and Kumaon. What the mission intended to do was nothing short of sacrilege. In a cruel twist of fate, the expedition that was sent to place the device was hit by bad weather and avalanches and it managed to lose the device somewhere on the glacier of the Nanda Devi. It lies there, buried deep in the snow, with the real danger of eroding and releasing poisonous plutonium in the very waters that make the Ganga. And the Indian government had no choice but to close the sanctuary.

One can debate endlessly about how true this story is, but the fact is that the Bhotiyas lost out on what they considered their birthright. The unilateral decision for closure without any community consultation, was the final straw that led to a long and bitter war of attrition between the locals and the government. It continues to date, although some important decisions have gone in favour of the locals. They now have the exclusive rights to manage the newly-opened trekking routes in and around the sanctuary and have organised themselves into a commercial entity to do exactly that. We were trekking with this group, the mountain shepherds.

Later in the afternoon, when the drizzle stopped and the clouds parted, we decided to go for a little exploration. We followed the stream and walked further ahead on the meadows. These same meadows, which were not even on the map, were once the halting place of so many caravans to and from Tibet. Traders would have camped here, their horses and yaks would have drunk from the stream and grazed on this grass. This place must have been buzzing with laughter and barter. The repercussions of war are usually felt most by those who never want it in the first place. The Niti Valley Bhotiyas lost their land, their way of life, their identity … for someone else's war. Trekking is allowing them a way back.

THE GUIDE

The Niti Valley and Auli, at its entry point, have some good trekking options. Auli also has fantastic skiing slopes in winter. Till Joshimath, the roads and guesthouses are jam-packed during season time, but beyond Joshimath, Niti Valley stays untouched. Auli is also popular during summer as a day trip from Joshimath, but it is in winter that it really comes into its own. GMVN, the tourist department of Garhwal, conducts skiing training here, and if you want to learn, there can't be a better place.

ITINERARY 10: SKIING IN AULI

Category: Skiing holiday.

Recommended for: Those who want to learn the basics of skiing.

Who can do this: All age groups, but need good fitness levels.

How long: 7 to 9 days.

When: January to March.

- Day 1: Reach Haridwar / Dehradun by train / flight. Long drive to reach Joshimath.
- Day 2: Take the cable car to Auli. It takes a long time by road, which is anyway likely to be closed due to snow. Can either register for a course or just stay there and take private lessons.
- Days 3–5: Give yourself at least three days to get the hang of skiing and reach the higher slopes. If doing the course, you need to stay for a week, minimum.
- Day 6: Cable car back and the drive back to Kaudiyala, about 30 km before Rishikesh. Stay in a river camp.
- Day 7: A white water rafting session, followed by lunch and drive back to Haridwar or Dehradun for train / flight.

ITINERARY 11: DAMARSAIN MEADOWS TREK

Category: Short, easy trek.

Recommended for: Those who want to explore, but also take it easy.

Who can do this: All age groups, basic fitness levels.

How long: 7 days.

When: May to October.

- Day 1: Reach Haridwar / Dehradun by train / flight. Drive to Rudraprayag / Srinagar or a similar midway place on the road to Joshimath.
- Day 2: Drive and reach Auli.
- Day 3: Do a short hike around Auli to acclimatise and also see the stunning views.
- Day 4: Long drive to reach Ghamsali village. Camp just ahead.
- Day 5: Trek to Damarsain meadows and camp there.
- Day 6: Back to Ghamsali and drive back to Joshimath or a little ahead.
- Day 7: Drive back to Dehradun / Haridwar for flight / train.

ITINERARY 12: THE NANDA DEVI SANCTUARY TREK

Category: Trek

Recommended for: Trekkers who don't like crowded trails.

Who can do this: Good fitness levels and / or prior trek experience.

How long: 9 days.

When: May to October, except during the monsoon.

- Days 1–3: Same as Itinerary 11.
- Day 4: Drive to Lata village and start the trek from there.
- Days 4–8: Trek till Dharansi Pass to see the inner sanctuary from the legendary route of Shipton and Tillman.
- Day 8: Back to Lata village (or Surai village via Tolma route) and drive back to Joshimath or a little ahead.
- Day 9: Drive back to Dehradun / Haridwar for flight / train.

LOCAL CONTACTS

1. Mountain Shepherds is the authorised organisation for treks in the Niti Valley. They also have a base in Auli. Contact http://mountainshepherds.com/
2. GMVN runs ski-training courses in Auli during winter. http://gmvn.gov.in/

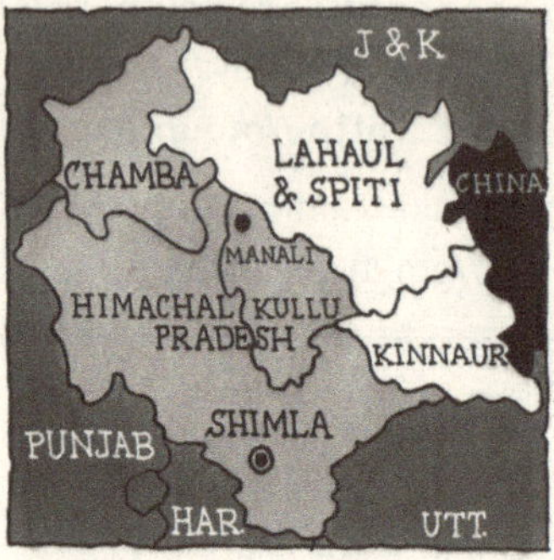

Hand-drawn maps for representation purposes only.
Not to scale.

KHAN PARI PASS

Hidden in plain sight

Manali evokes two diametrically opposite reactions. There are people whose ultimate goal in life is to go to Manali, sight-see, chill in coffee shops, maybe have a joint … And then there are those who cringe at the mere mention of the name—it's too crowded, too loud and full of people with no love for the mountains. Both these groups miss out on Manali, the one beyond the obvious. Make no mistake, there is so much around Manali that is still undiscovered, and one of those 'hidden in plain sight' type treks is to the Khan Pari Pass. Just the name is reason enough for you to want to go for this trek. It surely was for me and a group of friends in the monsoon of 2015. That's another thing about Manali, or for that matter, most of the Himalaya—it is at its best during the rains, when the least number of people go there. This is an account of our trek and our time in the mountains amidst clouds and flowers.

Monsoon in the Himalaya

'No wonder people don't come to the mountains in the monsoon,' Aparna summarised our twenty-four-hour ordeal to reach Manali in a sentence. Actually, it was not really the monsoon's fault—it was our optimism against odds. We took the flight option from Delhi to Kullu in August, knowing how unlikely it was that the flight would take off (flights to Kullu usually get cancelled as it is one of the most difficult airstrips to land on and needs full visibility conditions). But it did take off and we were delighted. We gave each other examples of how we must always try our luck, took pictures of Kullu Valley from the window and were on a high until the point when the captain announced that the weather conditions were not conducive for landing and that we had to head back to Delhi. After an initial display of disappointment, we were resigned to our fate. But we were young, this was an impromptu plan, we were not bound by a fixed schedule, and by the time we landed we were in high spirits again. We planned to hire a traveller and drive all the way to Kullu. Optimistic again, but who said optimism gets tempered after one bad experience?

After a couple of long breaks for lunch and tea, it was past 10 p.m. and we were still four hours away from Manali. And it was raining. We decided to spend the night at a roadside hotel and leave early in the morning, the first sensible decision we had taken in the last twelve hours. Then began the round of knocking on closed doors, waking up sleepy watchmen, shouting over the din of rain and thunder and asking for rooms. We got lucky on our fifth attempt, and within ten minutes we were asleep in whatever rooms we could get. Like it usually is after a rainy night, the morning was nice and clear. We managed to wake up early, had some tea and toast, and got back on the road. We reached in what seemed like no time, and found a 'gleaming in the mid-morning sun' Manali. Empty roads, shops opening reluctantly for another slow business day, just a few tourists with their backpacks—it was as if we had time travelled back to the '80s.

If you stand in the middle of Mall Road in Manali and look up at any side, the view will not be very different from what it would have been thirty years ago. Dense deodar forests on high mountains with clouds floating in their folds, villages with slate-roofed homes that look impossible to reach, dark green meadows … and peeking through the clouds, snow-covered peaks. It is immensely beautiful, and it only gets enhanced during the monsoon. The first decision we took after reaching Manali, and our second good one in a row, was to spend an extra day here before starting our trek. Manali had gotten us, hook, line and sinker.

A fairy tale land above Hadimba

Two days passed just like that. We stayed indoors when it rained and roamed around when it was clear. Everything was slow and unplanned, the opposite of our lives back in Mumbai. And then it was time for the trek. Manali and the villages towards the north and east of it are the starting point for many popular treks—Beas Kund, Hampta Pass, to name just two. But the area right above Manali, towards the west, had somehow managed to slip off the map. It's called the Manali Sanctuary and no one seems to go there. This was evident from our struggle to find guides who knew the routes for treks in that region. We finally went ahead with a local couple who ran a trekking agency and had some knowledge about this region. But it was right above the Hadimba temple, one of the most-visited spots of Manali. You just have to look up towards the dense forest above Hadimba and wonder what lies beyond. A world of undiscovered fantastic trails, that's what.

The trek started with us climbing through the thick forest above the Hadimba temple. No getting used to the conditions, no taking it easy, straight on to the struggle. Maybe this is what has kept everyone away from this trek, we thought. But you can't wonder much on uphill climbs. Your thoughts are drowned by the thudding of your heart in your ears. After every two steps you look up, only to realise that you are still pretty much where you were. The big advantage we had though (see how the perspective changes), was that it was monsoon. So the sun was behind the clouds and it was cool. The thought of a steep climb under a hot sun was enough for us to keep going and not crib. That, and the fact that it was an unusually diverse forest. Lord Brahma's creativity was in full display and every possible inch was covered with a shade of green. Short grass, medium grass, tall grass, very tall grass, short trees, big trees, very big trees … there was everything, and all together. And when we climbed a little higher, we entered the fog and into this fairy tale land where we stayed for the next three days.

The first feature of a fairy tale land is that it's cut-off from the world you know. The thick clouds all around us ensured that. Another feature is the fantastical things that you could not imagine exist: grass which was taller than us, fields of flowers, mist that engulfed us from inside and out, there were many. Not expected, but gladly accepted. Our shoes got soaked just by walking on trails that were no longer visible under the wild growth. Prakash, the trek leader, who was walking in front, had to hack at the grass with a machete—it was like we were in the Amazon. The only place where we could take a break was on a rocky outcrop and that became our lunch spot. We had aloo parantha with pickle while surrounded by mist and the mad, crazy grass. Prakash pointed at the clouds below us and told us that, on a clear day, there would have been a direct view of Manali. Ya, whatever, we thought. Once upon a time we liked Manali, now we loved this world. We were just three hours away.

After lunch, we started off again, the trail less steep now, but the grass even taller. The hacking-happy guide gave up too. How much can you fight nature? We were amazed that he could see the trail at all (if this was the trail). It felt like we were climbing straight through the densest vegetation ever (picture on page x of the inserts). We couldn't see each other or the guides. They were guiding us by sound. 'Yellow flower se left ...' and so on. When the grass wasn't taller than us, we saw tonnes and tonnes of flowers and we walked through them. The trekking was easy now, the weather was cool and we knew what to expect. By 4 p.m., we reached the small clearing of Lama Dug, at 2,800 metres, and our Day 1 campsite. The tents were pitched on knee-high grass (the shortest since morning), including a dining tent, which became our adda for the rest of the evening. Laughter and stories over chai and pakoras filled the misty air of Lama Dug. There was a constant drizzle all evening and all night, but it stopped just when it was time to get going the next morning.

HISTORY AND MYTH-MAKING IN THE HIMALAYA

—A note by Bill Aitken

If the variety of geographic features, geological finds, birds, butterflies and plant species attract our attention, so should the pages of history. But in the domain of Puranic lore, history fights a losing battle against myth-making.

In Frazer's 1815 map of my home area, Mussoorie, the town finds no mention, since it did not come into existence till 1828. When the British came, the surrounding hills were mainly grasslands. Hence, most of today's oak jungles, sown by them, have trees of slender girth. Up until motorable roads came, the oaks were lopped for fodder to feed the family buffalo which then would supply the town with milk. Now milk vans ply the roads and the oaks are spared. In addition, the oak trees provided the wood for walking sticks, and this souvenir trade has now been stopped by the Forest Department. Across the Aglar Valley are fine stands of the fragrant deodar on the prominent bulk of Nag Tibba, where wild boar rootle, bears grunt and, in season, Gujjar herders graze buffalo and make ghee and kheer. Wrapped in two layers of plastic, there is no softer (or more edible) pillow than that fashioned from five kilos of rice pudding.

Nag Tibba was the route taken by the Austrian mountaineer Heinrich Harrer on his so-called escape to Tibet. To prove how historical fact is no match for myth, Harrer's real character continues to be obscured by Mussoorie tourists' wishful thinking. Harrer's remarkable journey from an internment camp in Dehradun to Lhasa is recounted with skill—and deceit—in his bestselling book, *Seven Years in Tibet*. The book's blurb asks us to believe Harrer was 'an Olympic ski-champion who with an almost super-human effort, succeeded in escaping to become the first Westerner to lay eyes on Lhasa'. In reality, there were no Olympic games, though Harrer was a ski instructor (of decidedly murky purpose) for the Gestapo. He had no need to escape since, as an Austrian, the British offered him freedom from internment (a fact that he hides) and which, as a Nazi, he refused. Harrer was not the first Westerner to lay eyes on Lhasa—he was the thirty-first. Concealed from the public is the fact that the Lhasa regent invited the Third Reich to send thirty Nazi anthropologists to visit Lhasa in 1938.

Harrer's greatest achievement was not in climbing the Eiger Nordwand nor in trekking to Tibet, but in his effrontery as an artful dodger in successfully making suckers of us five million readers of his book which covers up a shameful Nazi past that the author was not man enough to face.

• • •

To Khan Pari Pass

Day 2 started on familiar terms. A climb through fog, thick grass and lots and lots of flowers. Yellow, blue, violet, orange, red, every single colour vied for attention. At times like this, you regret not paying attention in botany class.

All we could do was count the colours, sizes and shapes of flowers—we didn't know their names or any other details. The trail kept climbing around the mountain and finally, at around 3,200 metres, we crossed the tree line and were in open land. We were now behind the mountain that we could see from Manali, and in uncharted territory. Shortly, we came upon a point where the trail split. The main trail continued ahead to Bara Banghal, one of the most challenging but fascinating treks in the Himalaya. A narrower, less used trail turns left towards the Khan Pari Pass. The guides had all been to Bara Banghal, but only one old guide had been to Khan Pari Pass, many years ago, and he had but a foggy memory of his trip.

It might not be a known trail, but it was stunning. Rolling green slopes full of flowers, and through them, a trail climbing steadily up. As we started walking uphill, the fog also started clearing a bit and we could see the wide expanse all around us. A picture will help you understand better (on page x of the inserts). The clouds also parted for a moment and we saw the giant, snow-covered mountains of the Bara Banghal range to our right, beyond which lies the mythical village of Bara Banghal. Just getting there requires four days of difficult trekking over a high pass. We were not in a position to appreciate those difficulties though—our own struggles were keeping us occupied. As is the case for most passes, even the not very high ones like the Khan Pari, the climb was relentless. No flat patch and no chance of steadying our breath. Up and up we went for what seemed like forever. The fog played hide and seek, and just when we were about to reach the top, it cleared. At 12.30 p.m., after four hours and about 1,000 metres of climbing, we were at the topmost part of the trail, the Khan Pari Pass.

We were thrilled of course, because 'no more climbing', but also because we were venturing into the unknown. The trail ended at Khan Pari Pass, and beyond this it was uncharted territory. But first, it was time to celebrate the ascent to Khan Pari Pass. Out came our lunchboxes and we had delicious puris with aloo sabzi and pickle. Then we decided to rest for fifteen minutes. It was a rare chance to chill at the top of a pass. Usually you get up there and rush down. But it wasn't so high, we were in no hurry, there was a nice slope with soft grass perfect for lounging, and it wasn't windy yet … all conditions conducive for a siesta. Do check the picture on page x of the inserts. But no matter how different this pass was from the others we had crossed, there was one similarity. A crucial one at that. The weather changes within minutes. In less than ten minutes of us resting there, the wind picked up, the fog came back and the temperature dropped. All signs that we had to pack up and leave.

The guides were tense and having a discussion with Prakash. It was obviously about what path to take downhill from there. As I mentioned, there was no trail beyond this point. But more importantly, the fog had really thickened. It was a proper white out. Perfect conditions to get lost on a trail, let alone descend without a trail. But the longer we waited at the top, the thicker the fog was getting and the colder it was becoming. It was decided that we do the descent to campsite in two parts. Part 1—we go down the slope, staying as close as possible to each other, following the voice cues of the guides. We would do this in three separate rows, each led by a guide and two to three of us behind each guide, staying within visible distance. The aim was to reach a small lake called Rani Sui. Part 2 was a shorter, easier walk to the campsite. The guides got their whistles out, we made three rows, identified our row-mates and on the count of three, we started.

To Rani Sui

But we forgot to discuss whether we were to run or walk. The natural tendency is to run down such beautiful grassy slopes, and within five minutes we had scattered all over the hillside, some running down, others walking and sticking to their partners. Take a moment to look at this picture on page xi of the inserts to get an idea of the conditions. Every time we glanced back to check on the others, we lost track of which direction we were heading down. There was no such thing as straight down, as the slopes were not necessarily uniform and could take you in different directions. However, no matter what, all slopes eventually lead downwards. That was the only saving grace. That, and the sudden appearance of a Gaddi shepherd.

If you have read the Kugti Pass story in Chapter 4, you know who they are. If you haven't yet, well they are one of the semi-nomadic shepherd communities of the Himalaya. They stay in the high meadows during the entire summer with their sheep, and come down in winter. This Gaddi, Uday, we later found out, had been staying in the meadows around Khan Pari Pass with his flock of 1,000 sheep and two sheep dogs for the last three months. He would be here for another two at least. He had been following this routine for the last many years. Fog or no fog, he knew every inch of this land, every rock, every meadow, every pond. It was his whistle that we had heard when most of us had come down the slope and were scattered all over. The guides immediately started a communication channel, whistling back. None of us could see him, but he could see us, with his Gaddi eyes.

Over a series of whistles and shouts back and forth, he communicated the route to us. He was somewhere below us in the fog, we could make out that much. Gradually, all of us gathered and began walking together. Another twenty minutes or so, and we saw a big depression in front of us. The Rani Sui lake. A pond actually, it is nevertheless a significant landmark in this unmapped region. Legends tell of a queen who loved to visit this lake and bathe here. Sui, in local language, is a pond. The queen's pond. Must have been one hell of an adventurous queen to choose this place. When we reached there, it was still a complete white out so we couldn't see the view the queen must have enjoyed while bathing. But we were content, nonetheless. We'd had an unexpectedly exciting day, not so tough, never in real danger, but still thrilling, one we enjoyed. From here onwards, there were undulating meadows for the next 2 km and we could camp anywhere, Kishenji the old guide told us. He, Prakash and the rest of us had almost forgotten about the unseen Gaddi, when he chose to make an appearance.

The Gaddi, his sheep and his kingdom

Just a dark shadow in the fog first, he soon appeared in full glory, smiling shyly, a blanket on his shoulder, a Himachali cap on his head, a stick in hand, and a dog following him. The lord of these lands. All of us looked at him, and there was total silence. He ventured closer to us and then just sat on a rock, waving out to the guides. Nonchalantly cool. We thanked him for his help and asked about him. He told us about his 1,000 sheep and his daily routine. His sheep were out grazing now and would return by 5 p.m., at which time he would gather them together and settle them for the night, before making his dinner and settling down for the night himself. His camp was about 2-3 km from here, he said. His dogs would help him with the sheep and also give him company. The Gaddis allocate the meadows between themselves and there was no other shepherd around for kilometres. Once a month, someone would come up, bring rations and news, if any. 'Time passes quite nicely, and I never get bored,' he told us. We obviously couldn't fathom his way of life. The next generation didn't aspire to be shepherds anymore, he said. But sheep are their only wealth, and if there are sheep, they need to be taken to the mountains to graze. Only time will tell what happens to the Gaddis.

The guides invited him to come along with us till the campsite and have tea, which he happily agreed to. We started on a beautiful walk through the meadows, no up or down anymore, just flat. And after half an hour, we stopped at a spot which had a small water body nearby, flat ground to pitch tents and a beautiful view (once the fog cleared the next morning), according to the Gaddi.

This became our Day 2 campsite. Uday had his tea and disappeared into the fog once again. Like the Gaddi's sheep, we also now settled down for the night. There was tea and pakora again for the evening, followed by games and chatting in the dining tent. Then followed a wholesome dinner of rice, dal, roti, sabzi, plus a special dessert, and by 9 p.m., we were all inside our sleeping bags, thinking about a way of life that is so alien to us only because we are so disconnected from nature.

True to the Gaddi's word, the morning was brighter. The clouds above us and the fog around us were dissipating. Through the gaps, we saw some stunning scenery. The snow-covered giants of the Pir Panjal range to our right, the wide Kullu Valley below us and miles of beautiful meadows to our left. By the time we brushed and changed, it was even clearer. The clearest it had been since we had taken the first step on the trek. Our eyes can only appreciate beauty to a certain extent, beyond that it is overwhelming. That's what happened to us. We kept shaking our heads in disbelief, running from left to right, trying to capture what we saw in panorama mode, telling each other to not miss that or this. Usually, the guides and porters have a good laugh at us city people behaving like we have seen heaven, but in this case, they were on our side. Prakash was trying to identify the names of the snow peaks, Deo Tibba and Hanuman Tibba being the most prominent ones. Even the Rohtang Pass could be seen. The breakfast table was also set out in the open today, to celebrate a morning without fog. Check out the picture on page xi of the inserts.

The best though, was reserved for last. Far off to our

left, the fog was now lifting, and once it cleared, we saw hundreds of sheep spread out on the meadows. Uday's sheep. Clouds floating above and in the folds of the high mountains and lush green meadows below. It was a sight which is so tough to explain—it was that mind-blowingly beautiful. Even the picture on page xi of the inserts can do little justice.

'Ya, I can see why he is content here,' Maanuv thought out loud. At all times, we were aware that we were only a one-and-a-half day walk from Manali, and that made it even more special. This fairy tale land, this kingdom of the Gaddis. Accessible, but not appreciated, like the wisdom of a grandmother.

When the kingdom was resplendent in its full glory, how could the king not make an appearance? Uday soon joined us again at the camp. The guides teased him about missing us—he just smiled back. He mingled with us more freely today, had a bit of our breakfast and then sat down at the edge of the meadow to enjoy the view of Kullu and Manali. Rujuta sat beside him and took his interview (and that's how we know what we know about him). The two true mountain lovers sitting side by side, at one with the surroundings, presented a perfect picture and you should see it on page xii of the inserts. After he'd had his fill, he got up, smiled again, waved and left. The rest of us lazed around in the morning sun and just soaked it all in. Prakash finally had to intervene and remind us that a long day lay ahead, even though it was all downhill. He then sheepishly added that they would have to find the trail as well. We were still in unknown territory.

Through the unknown

After a quick pack up and a stretch, we were ready and waiting for the guides to lead. Just then, in less than five minutes, the fog factories hidden in the Himalaya kicked into overdrive. We were engulfed in thick fog all over again. 'Where does it come from and where does it go,' should be the signature tune of the Himalayan fog. The guides looked worried. The known trail lay 4 km away, and in between, there was just open land full of meadows, snow patches and rocky outcrops. Even on a clear day, they would have struggled to find the trail. Now with the fog, it had become extremely difficult, to say the least. We could make out that, this time, our safety was at stake. We started walking, slowly and carefully. But the fog only thickened further, and even the prominent markers that the old guide knew were no longer visible. There was a serious silence, broken only by the arguments between the guides about the right direction. The snow patches and slippery rocks were a big concern and we were told to wait while Prakash and the old guide went ahead to scout. We waited for about fifteen minutes, ears on high alert, but nothing. The remaining guides were now worried for the two who had gone ahead. It was tense stuff, and something needed to happen fast.

Something did happen. A figure approached us through the fog.

'I will take you to the trail,' a soft voice said in Hindi. Uday! In his signature style. We didn't even recognise him till he was right next to us, even though we knew that he was the only human being apart from us in this entire region. He returned because he had figured that we might need help once the fog thickened. And boy, did we. And so started the most thrilling stretch of trekking we had ever done. Blindly following Uday—we couldn't see anything anyway—we walked in single file behind him. Along the narrow edge of snow patches, across rocky patches and through thick grass, he took us slowly but surely down the mountain. At one point he stopped, asked us to wait, went ahead a bit, came back and told us that Prakash and the guide had gone the wrong way. So now, we had to look for them too. By 'we', I mean 'he'. He continued to lead the way, and at the same time kept an eye out for them. To get an idea of the terrain and conditions, you must check this picture on page xii of the inserts. We finally heard their shouts and Uday shouted back, giving them instructions as to how to get back on the route. A relieved Prakash and Kishenji met us ten minutes later.

Another half an hour and we were on the trail. Uday pointed to a thick jungle some distance away and told us that we needed to get there. He had saved us. He had walked 4 km, and would now walk back 4 more, just like that. Without him, I have no idea how we would have come down the slippery mountain. In characteristic Gaddi style, he downplayed his role, wished us well and quickly turned around. Only our loud protests stopped him. He agreed to share a bit of our snacks. After having some dry fruits and nuts, and getting some pictures clicked, he got up, waved goodbye and disappeared back into the fog.

'Is he even for real? I mean he is not one of those friendly spirits you talk about na, GP?' Aparna asked, as soon as he had gone.

'Let's check the camera on which we clicked his picture. If he is not real, there will be no picture,' suggested Sneha.

'What nonsense,' Nitin replied, but he was already unsure. And we actually checked the camera. This is what we saw (on page xii of the inserts).

The mystery of Shankchar

Once on the trail, it was easier. We were coming down steadily and kept an eye on the forest in the distance. In about an hour, as we got closer, we sensed that there was something eerie about the place. The kind of feeling you get when you are somewhere no one goes. The meadow was unkempt, no sheep had grazed here for a long time, the forest was dark and full of dead trees, no one had picked wood here recently either. The old guide, who was finally on familiar terrain, and had found his voice, asked us to come closer.

'There is a reason there is no trail here,' he said, '… even though it's so close to the village, which in turn is close to the highway.'

'Wait, let's sit down and have our lunch, and then you tell us,' I requested. A hungry stomach can't pay attention. We sat down in a circle, took out our lunch boxes, and over pulao and pickle, listened to the story of Shankchar village.

Shankchar is a small village, right below the thick

forest in front of us. Like all high Himalayan villages, the inhabitants were completely dependent on agriculture for their livelihood. However, the forest was protected and good land was difficult to find. More difficult than in the other villages at least. So, the villagers decided to, or rather were forced to, grow poppy in hidden fields. Just where the forest ended and the meadows began, they flattened some land and started growing poppy, which is illegal in the Himalaya. To keep this hidden, they deliberately spread stories about the forest being dangerous and about it being haunted by evil spirits, etc. They ensured that the trail through the forest was ill-kept, so that it became tough for anyone to climb up or down. They also ensured that shepherds kept away from the meadows above the village. All this, so that they could make ends meet. It was one of those situations which are morally ambiguous. We decided that, since we had no clue about the struggles of the villagers, we would keep our judgements to ourselves.

'Just tell us there are no evil spirits,' Sneha begged.

'No, but there are bears,' Kishenji replied.

It was time to walk through this dark, strange forest. Usually, it's a delight to walk through a forest, but this was an ordeal. The trail was broken at almost every corner. We constantly slipped and fell, getting pricked by thorns which grew right next to the trail. Suddenly, Prakash, who was walking in front, stopped and put a finger on his lips. Silence. We had no clue what it was about but looked all around us just like he did, slowly inching closer to each other. After a couple of minutes of high tension, he gestured for us to step ahead and look at the trail. Bang in the middle were the fresh footmarks of a bear.

'It has walked here less than fifteen minutes ago. Must have heard us coming,' Prakash told us softly.

'Now what?' someone asked.

'Nothing. We keep going, keep making loud sounds and get down fast.'

Easier said than done. This crazy trail, full of wild zig-zags, thorny bushes, slippery rocks and steep descents, was not at all conducive for 'getting down fast'. But, the presence of a wild bear surely was.

Bruised, battered and stung, we finally got down the worst part of the trail. Closer to the village, the path was better and wider. We met a couple of villagers going up, who, after their initial surprise, smiled at us (instead of, I don't know, cutting out our tongues so that we couldn't tell the world), and told us that we were brave to do this trek.

'Don't cross this forest after evening,' one of them warned us.

Soon, we reached the village and normalcy. People were doing the usual village things. Children were running around with their school bags still on their backs. Men were sitting around and chatting, surely about politics and Obama, while women were busy filling water, carrying wood, doing real work. All signs of normalcy. We let go of our apprehensions and decided to celebrate the finish of the trek. High fives were exchanged and sweets were shared. Trek end pictures were clicked. Backpacks came off and shoes were replaced with slippers.

'Kahan se aaye ho?' a voice asked.

We looked around but couldn't see anyone.

'Upar dekho.'

On the top of a slate roof, three old women were sitting and enjoying the sun. They gestured for us to climb up too. It's tradition. So we climbed and sat with the wise old ladies of the Himalaya. Picture on page xii of the inserts. They called for tea and we shared whatever food we had. Sitting atop a slate roof, sipping on sweet pahadi chai, listening to the uninhibited laughter of the old women, we knew that all was well with the world.

THE GUIDE

You are spoilt for choices in Manali. Adventure activities, treks, short walks, temple trails, and much more. Here are two itineraries, with the main aim of avoiding the crowds.

ITINERARY 13: THE NAGGAR TEMPLE TRAIL

Category: Short walks.

Recommended for: History buffs, off-beat travellers.

Who can do this: Everyone, age and fitness levels no bar.

How long: 5 days.

When: Throughout the year; best during monsoon and winter.

- Day 1: Reach Naggar either by flying into Kullu (one hour) or driving from Chandigarh (nine hours).
- Day 2: Daily walks to explore Naggar and the beautiful temples all around. Start the first day with a walk in the village of Naggar itself, with its beautiful old homes and many temples, especially the Tripura Sundari. Also, the famous Nicholas Roerich gallery. And the temple at Thava.
- Day 3: A walk to Rumsu village. You can walk even further to the amazing forest above it.
- Day 4: A visit to Manali if you want to see the madness. Or another easy day at Naggar.
- Day 5: Return via Kullu or Chandigarh.

ITINERARY 14: KHAN PARI PASS TREK

Category: Short trek.

Recommended for: First-time trekkers.

Who can do this: Everyone, basic fitness levels.

How long: 6 days.

When: Summer and monsoon.

- Day 1: From Kullu or Chandigarh, drive to Naggar (if season time) or Manali (if off-season).
- Day 2: Spend a day in Naggar or Manali, just chilling, walking around.
- Days 3–5: Trek to Khan Pari Pass and finish close to the highway near Kullu. If you want to splurge, stay in Span resorts, or else at Naggar castle.
- Day 6: Return via Kullu or Chandigarh.

Don't miss—Parashar lake

On the highway to Manali, as you reach Mandi, take a diversion and head towards Parashar lake. It's a hidden gem (actually, not so much anymore) and a quick dekho is worth the effort. You can also go there specifically to camp, or in winter to see the lake frozen and surrounded by snow.

Don't miss—Thava

Naggar was the ancient capital of Kullu Valley. Before it was Naggar, it was Thava. A once-flourishing town, it was destroyed by an earthquake. The only remaining structure is the beautiful temple of Krishna, tilting to its left. A short walk from Naggar.

LOCAL CONTACTS

1. We used the services of Himalayan Challenges for the Khan Pari Pass trek. They organise mountain biking trips too. Contact http://himalayanchallenges.com/
2. HPTDC, the state tourism department, has some of the best places to stay in Himachal, especially the Naggar castle. http://hptdc.in/

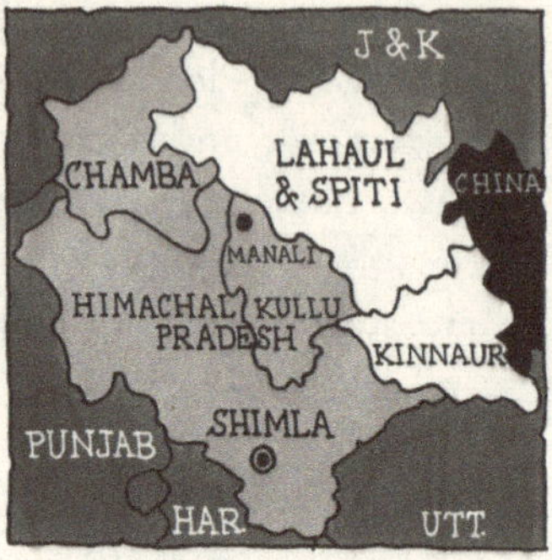

Hand-drawn maps for representation purposes only.
Not to scale.

KALPA AND SANGLA

Wanderings in Kinnaur

Your best-laid plans rarely come off in the high Himalaya. But rarely do your plans not come off at all. In 2010, we went for the Kinner Kailash trek in Kinnaur. Kinner Kailash is one of the mythical homes of Shiva, and a perambulation of this mountain is part of the local culture and amongst the most challenging pilgrimages in the world. The trek follows the same route and it required plenty of planning and preparation. All of us were clear that the itinerary, as we had planned it, would alter in some way or another. What we had not imagined was that things would take such a turn that we would not be able to reach the starting point of the trek. But through a series of events, we re-learnt a very important lesson—the Himalaya gives back much more than it takes. This is an account of our failed trek to Kinner Kailash, but a successful trip to the Himalaya.

Gathering of the gods

The rainbow we will never forget is the one that greeted us as we pulled into the Kalpa market that evening, floating high amidst the Kinner Kailash range. All ten of us, the two drivers and Negiji, our guide from Kalpa, got out of the cars and stared till it lasted. We almost forgot to capture it, so mesmerised were we. But we managed to click one photograph, just before it disappeared and you can see it on page xiii of the inserts. The rainbow did two things: it uplifted our mood after a day-long drive in gloomy, overcast conditions, and it answered the inevitable question of why we were staying in Kalpa.

Kalpa, the erstwhile capital of Kinnaur, lies perched on the side of a huge mountain directly facing the magnificent Kinner Kailash range, less than 10 km as the crow flies. It is so close that you feel like running across the valley and touching the eternal snows. So close, that even inside the restaurant of the guesthouse we checked into, we had to wear sunglasses because of the snow glare. But the short burst of sunlight was a red herring. By evening, the clouds came back from wherever they had gone for a break and settled in for a long innings. It rained the entire night, and when we woke up the next morning, it was still raining. With every passing hour, as the rain persisted, the town of Kalpa went into collective despair. The apple crop of the entire region, its main source of income, was just a week away from ripening, and so much rain would spell doom.

THE SNOW IS DISAPPEARING

This was September. It wasn't supposed to rain like this, that's why we had chosen this time for the trek. But weather patterns everywhere in the Himalaya are going haywire. In winter, it doesn't snow as much as it used to, and in summer there are crazy rains like never before. For people who are so dependent on the weather, this is nothing short of life-threatening. Their crops get destroyed in the unseasonal hailstorms, their streams dry up when they need water the most, the roads are blocked for days when they need medical help, the list is endless.

For thousands of years, the natives have managed to live in harmony with the elements, understanding the fragility of their environment. They observed and figured patterns and wove their lives around it. And just in the last ten years, all that wisdom has been invalidated. World leaders can continue to meet for climate change summits, but the Himalaya needs saving now. You can do your bit. Switch off electricity when you don't need it, use water conservatively, car pool or use public transportation or just walk more. Every small step counts.

• • •

Sombre crowds could be seen everywhere—in the guesthouse, at the roadside tea stalls, inside parked cars. Utterly and completely dependent on the weather, we wondered what these people would do now. But we didn't account for their gods. Every small village in the Himalaya, especially in Himachal and Uttarakhand, has a resident devi or devta. Till date, every important matter—question, advice or dispute—is put forth to them and theirs is usually the final say. And when there is an issue of collective importance, or something which a single devi / devta cannot handle, they get together and discuss. This was one such time. In the small ground of Kalpa town, as soon as there was a break in the rain, the devis and devtas of all the nearby villages were to gather, to discuss the situation and give their verdict.

The gods, all dressed up, are usually brought out of the temples on their palanquins, with two or four men carrying them on their shoulders. We had once seen a ceremony in another small village in Kinnaur, where the local devta was asked questions of all kinds ('Will I pass my 10th exam?', 'Should I grow apple this year?', etc.) by the villagers. The devta was on the palanquin and the two men were constantly moving, rhythmically. When the question was asked, they would move in one way or another to denote a 'yes' or a 'no'.

'How do the two men decide which way to move?' we asked our host.

'The devta decides, and they convey,' he answered. There was no way for the two men to know what the devta was going to answer, so there was little likelihood of this being a staged act. The question had to be framed in a way that it could be answered in a 'yes' or a 'no'. We found the answers in most cases to be practical, and whenever the question was one for which there was no easy answer, the devta did not give one.

That evening, when the rain stopped for a short time, even though the clouds still looked menacing, we went to the town centre. Sitting in the middle of the ground, all by themselves, were the gods on their palanquins, in deep discussion. Check the picture on page xiii of the inserts. Hundreds of people were standing silently on the sidelines. A verdict was expected anytime soon, someone told us. We were all fascinated, but the non-believers amongst us were like, 'What does this mean? How will they announce the verdict?'

'Through an interpreter,' someone told us. There are designated interpreters who can understand what the devtas have to say, and put it in words for everyone else. Suddenly, trumpets were blown loudly and there was a perceptible buzz in the air. A crowd of people gathered around the gods and soon the word spread—'The rain will stop within twelve hours, the apples will survive.'

The relieved crowd dispersed quickly, the gods were carried back to their homes, and we walked back slowly to the guesthouse, lost in our thoughts. Would the people have accepted the verdict if it had been the opposite? How would they have felt? Maybe, not so bad. Equanimity in all situations is one of the hallmarks of the Himalayan folk. That's why they can survive, enjoy themselves actually, in really tough conditions. We have always observed this during all our Himalayan trips. We didn't know at the time, but we were soon going to experience it too.

The Kinner Kailash trek starts from the village of Lambar, a few kilometres from Kalpa, along the mighty Satluj. The entire stretch of Satluj within Kinnaur had been subjected to many ill-conceived hydel power projects. Constant tunnelling had weakened the already fragile mountain system. The unusually high rainfall was just the last straw. There had been multiple landslides all over Kinnaur since morning. The road was blocked. Even if the rain stopped in the next twelve hours, the damage had been done. We were stuck.

Wanderings in Kalpa

Negiji gave us the news in the evening. We were all on the terrace, going wild looking at the Kinner Kailash range through a break in the clouds.

'What do you mean, "stuck"?'

'No way to reach the starting point of the trek.'

'Let's just walk over the landslide.'

'There are way too many, and there are chances of more happening, too risky.'

'So what should we do?'

'Let's wait for a day and hope for a miracle.'

The clouds came back and blocked the Kinner Kailash, and our excitement dipped. Equanimity is tough. It rained through the night, but when we woke up, it was a magically clear morning. Blue skies, white snow on the ranges. The prophecy had come true. Our chances of going on the trek also improved. Plus, we had a beautiful day to actually go out and see Kalpa. Hope surged, we were excited again. Equanimity is tough.

The day was well spent as follows: after breakfast, we took a steep walk down to the Kalpa market to see the small monastery with the big prayer wheel. We then visited the girls' orphanage next door. It was neat, clean and well run, with support from the government and private donations. A plate of momos in one of the many tiny shops in the market followed. We then got into cars and drove 8 km to Roghi, the last village on this section of the old Hindustan-Tibet Road. Just before Roghi, the road is cut straight through the face of a mountain and the spot is infamous as 'suicide point' as there is a straight fall of more than 1,000 feet. Roghi also has beautiful views of the Kinner Kailash range and a small dispensary which sells ayurvedic medicines for one rupee. We returned to the guesthouse for lunch, and there was still no news about the landslides. After a short siesta, we played some games in the courtyard.

In the evening, we climbed up from the guesthouse to see another, older monastery. It had beautiful murals and a mind-blowing view of the mountains. The lone monk there asked us to wait a little longer and see the moon rise from behind the Kinner Kailash. We waited. The moon rose. Our trip was made, then and there. Picture on page xiii of the inserts.

We came down from the monastery with our hearts full. Even when Negiji gave us the news that the trek was impossible, that the roads would take a week to clear, our hearts just absorbed the sorrow, much like it did the joy a while back. Perhaps equanimity happens to you after a couple of days in the Himalaya.

A door closes, another opens

For a couple of months now, everyone in the group had been thinking about the trek. We had been reading about it, checking pictures online, imagining ourselves in Charang village and on the legendary descent to Chitkul village, all the way from the Charang Ghati Pass. And now, here we were in Kalpa, the mountain right in front of us, but out of bounds. At least ten times that night we must have used the term 'so close, yet so far'. I mean, it really was no exaggeration. But the day in Kalpa had been quite fulfilling; the weather had been clear and was supposed to stay good. We were in a positive frame of mind. So it was decided that we would make the best of the five to six days that we had in hand.

There are three roads from Kalpa. One goes towards Lambar and further towards the Tibet border and to Spiti. The other goes back towards Shimla, and the third goes to Sangla Valley. The only choice we had was to go to what is considered one of the most beautiful valleys in the entire Himalaya. Not a bad 'only choice' to have at all.

I had been there quite a few times already. It's one of those places which lives up to the billing, surpasses it actually. Not that anyone needed convincing, but I told them stories from my previous visits which kind of firmed up our plans even more. Calls were made to gather information. Negiji was on overdrive. He felt more bad for us than we ourselves did.

'I will ensure that you reach Sangla Valley,' he vowed, and left for the night.

Sharp at 7 a.m., he was back with news. Just 10 km before Sangla, there had been a massive landslide. But, thank God there was a 'but', the local people were crossing over the landslide and coming in and out. Local jeeps were available on both sides of the landslide, so if we were up for it, we could reach Sangla. We were up for it from the moment he said 'but'.

We got into two jeeps at 9 a.m. and began our journey. Our first destination was Karcham, the place where the Sangla River meets the Satluj, and from where we had to take the diversion towards Sangla.

DAMN!

MAN-MADE NATURAL DISASTERS

As we drove towards Sangla, the hydel power projects along the Satluj looked nothing short of devilish. There was very little benefit to justify the huge cost that the local people, the river and the mountains were bearing. As I write this, I can't help but think about the protests in Mumbai (yes, even in Mumbai we protest sometimes) against the train shed proposed in the Aarey forest. But here, in the Himalaya, entire mountains are broken, huge rivers are dammed and diverted, villages and valleys are inundated, daily life and livelihoods are shattered—and it happens as if it's inevitable.

'Dams are the symbols of progress', 'It's for the greater good', 'Clean energy', are some of the things those responsible for this tell themselves. Environmental degradation is just a nuisance that comes in the way of development. But what about the financial loss? That surely matters, right? The monetary loss due to a poorly-planned hydel power project in the higher Himalaya, is huge. To give one example—roads that are blocked due to landslides just when the cash crop is ready to be taken to the market are much more of a cost to the local economy than what cheap electricity can save. And this is just one factor.

Costs come in many forms, and they remain for

years after the projects are completed. To compulsorily end this on a positive note—there are ways to minimise the damage done by a hydel power project. Studies and reports are easily available, even in the public domain. For example, the detailed one by Pandit and Grumbine, 2012.

• • •

From Karcham, the cars took a left and entered Sangla Valley. The valley is narrow here, and as we went deeper, it slowly started opening up. Soon we were at the landslide. A queue of local jeeps was waiting for villagers to cross over. We were told that there were some jeeps on the other side too. We got out of the cars, slung our heavy backpacks over our shoulders, and started walking. Most of us had no clue what a landslide looked like up close, let alone crossed one. But everyone else was doing it, so we would too. Soon, the road we were walking on disappeared under a huge rubble of rocks, mud and uprooted trees—the landslide. A narrow path had been made by—who else—the BRO, the Army unit responsible for making and maintaining all Himalayan roads. We started off on the narrow path and soon reached the heart of the landslide. A massive pile-up of boulders led straight down to the Sangla River. See picture on page xiv of the inserts. Standing at various points on the way were BRO workers, wearing helmets and hand-holding people across the landslide.

The person in charge was a thin, tall Sardarji, with

a stick in hand. He was amazing, constantly shouting instructions and keeping everything moving. He was also overseeing the crossing of essential goods—food items, LPG cylinders—into the Sangla Valley. A few Nepali porters were carrying sacks full of potatoes, onions, etc., and were getting thirty rupees for each crossing. We were asked to follow them. One by one, trying our best to not look down at the roaring river, we negotiated the tricky landslide and reached the other side. There was a steady stream of locals coming from Sangla too—life must go on after all. More importantly, there were jeeps waiting for anyone who crossed over.

Wanderings in Sangla Valley

Now, here is the thing. Sangla Valley was cut off from the rest of the world. The only way in and out was across this landslide. There was no electricity and no mobile network, so we couldn't get in touch with anyone to book our stay. We went on pure hope. The last time I was there, I had seen a beautiful camp by the river. Now that the trek was not happening, and Negiji had very kindly agreed to not charge anything apart from the expenses he had already incurred, we decided to splurge. The only problem—we didn't know if the camp was open. The drivers also didn't know, so we decided to just try our luck.

We should have just known. Not only was the camp open, but the people running it were overjoyed to see us and gave us a big fat discount. We had the whole camp to ourselves. There was a badminton and a volleyball court, carom, many board games and tonnes of books to read.

As Stu says in *Hangover*, our luck had officially turned around. In the morning, we had been disappointed about the trek not happening, and clueless about where to go next. And now, we were lazing around on hammocks in the afternoon sun, in a lovely camp overlooking the beautiful mountains of the Sangla Valley, with the crystal clear river flowing next to us and an orchard of fully loaded apple trees all around. Oh, and by the way, we were requested by the camp guys to eat as many of these apples as possible, as they were ripe and would get spoilt if not consumed soon.

The first day passed with us just enjoying our new setting. As there were three more days to go, we sat with the camp guides and made a list of things to do and see. 'To do' were a couple of short day treks, and 'to see' were Chitkul village and Kamru Fort. All of us were itching to trek. The next morning after breakfast, taking with us one of the guides, we headed off to Rakcham Glacier. It was a perfect day trek—4 km each way, starting from a small village just above the camp, then through fields, forests, meadows and all the way to the snout of the glacier. (If you trek here in May, you can touch the glacier.) As we walked further into the Sangla Valley, it widened more and more and presented us with beautiful sights. The fields of Ogra, a local grain similar to wheat, fiery red in colour (picture on page xiv of the inserts), made it a picture-postcard trek. By afternoon, it became cloudy, but true to the prediction of the gods, it didn't rain. We crossed streams, just like we would have on the Kinner Kailash trek, met shepherds and their sheep, ate lunch in a beautiful meadow and had a proper trek waala feeling overall. With one difference. After the day was over, we returned to the luxuries of a set camp, including a hot shower in the attached bathrooms.

The next day was a walk to Kamru Fort. We crossed the Sangla River and walked on the main road to Kamru. The fort is built on a small hill which overlooks the whole Sangla Valley and was the perfect vantage point for the kings of Sangla to rule from. The alleyways leading up to the fort were stunning. It was full of cobbled streets, with some very old houses that had beautiful woodwork on the doors and windows. The main entrance of the fort has a beautiful Buddha statue and then, through a series of low doors, we walked inside and into an open courtyard, where important functions are conducted till date. The fort towers right behind, dark brown in colour, are made entirely of wood and stone. Check this picture on page xiv of the inserts. Tourists are not allowed beyond the courtyard, but you can see the beautiful wooden balcony on the second floor from where the queen must have enjoyed the views while sipping her tea. There is also a statue of Kamakhya Devi, apparently from Assam, and on special occasions it is brought out. It's not clear how old the fort is, but some estimate it to be from the fifteenth century. Overall, we felt that the Kamru Fort was a mixture of beautiful, unique architecture and history, and most importantly, not yet a tourist spot.

We got back to the camp for lunch and an afternoon siesta.

Later in the day, we went for a short walk above the camp towards the Sangla Kanda meadows. The meadows are a favourite spot for the local shepherds as they are close by and also perfect grazing grounds for the sheep. But today was not a grazing day. It was the once-a-month bathing day. And sheep hate taking a bath—our lesson for today. All the shepherds had gathered their sheep inside a pen just above the village. The only way out was through a narrow opening which led straight into a small tank full of water (mixed with an antiseptic). It was hilarious (for us, surely not for the sheep) to see the survival of the fittest being played out.

The sheep in front were pushing away from the tank, only to be pushed back by the others as there was no way out. The ones who realised the inevitability of the bath were jumping reluctantly into the tank and then quickly swimming across and getting out. When only half the sheep were left, and none of the rest was coming forward, the shepherds jumped in and had to physically lift and throw the remaining sheep into the tank. For their own good, they told us. Do see the picture on page xv of the inserts. It surely got us thinking about the need for a daily bath.

To the last village before Tibet

The last day in Sangla Valley dawned nice and bright, the clearest since we had started on this trip. The Himalaya was in a kind mood. After a lazy breakfast, we got into a couple of jeeps that we had hired the previous day from Kamru and started driving towards Chitkul, about 15 km away. At 3,450 metres, it's a very high village, but more importantly, it's the last village before the Tibet border. We would have finished our trek here, so it was only right that we were ending our Sangla stay with a visit to the village. Just a few kilometres before Chitkul, the cars suddenly stopped. What else but a landslide. But this was a small one. There was not enough space for the cars to pass, but we could go through easily. And that's what we did. It was such a delightful day that it was almost a crime not to walk. With the sound of the Sangla River in our ears, and snow-covered peaks in our sight, we had nothing to say as we walked towards Chitkul.

Before we saw Chitkul, we first saw their grain stores. And they looked beautiful. Called 'kuthaars', these structures are used to store food grains and also hay for winter, and are always located a bit away from the main village. Chitkul is completely snow-bound in the winter and these stores are critical. A little bit more walking and we could now see the beautiful, sprawling village. Located in the widest part of the Sangla Valley, surrounded by snow-covered mountains on three sides and with the river flowing next to it, this was a fairy tale village. The houses looked a level above all the other villages we had seen and there was an aura of prosperity here. There was a small 'hotel' which was open. We had tea and biscuits there, chatting with the locals who had gathered for news. Our original plan was to return to the camp for lunch, but such perfect days don't come so often. The hotel offered a meal of rajma-chawal, and we decided to walk up to Nagasthi.

If Chitkul was the last village before Tibet, Nagasthi, 2 km ahead, was the last place that civilians could go to. There is an ITBP (Indo-Tibetan Border Police) camp there, and on my previous trips we had always walked till there to say 'hi' to them. For the first kilometre, the trail passed through the fields of Chitkul and we got to know why it's a prosperous village—flat fertile land with an endless supply of water. The trail ahead was still flat, even though the altitude was high. We were now bang in the middle of the Greater Himalayan range and the high mountains—the meadows, the river and the glaciers were overwhelming (picture on page xv of the inserts). And soon we were at Nagasthi. Just before the camp, there is a helipad, one of the highest in this region. We sat there to take in the scenery. A small group of soldiers were walking towards us. When they got nearer, we all got up and saluted them. They had big smiles on their face and a big thermos with them. Tea.

And so the trip ended with us sharing laughter and hot tea with soldiers at a high camp, sitting on a beautiful meadow which also doubles up as a helipad, listening to the roar of the Sangla River, basking in the afternoon sun, surrounded by snow-covered peaks under a deep blue sky with not a single cloud on the horizon.

THE GUIDE

It's not an untouched valley anymore, but it still retains its charm. The long drive to get there is totally worth it just for the views. The experiences are extra. From the short walks described in the story above to proper treks, there is a lot to do here.

ITINERARY 15: THE SANGLA VALLEY ADVENTURE

Category: Road trip plus short walks.

Recommended for: Those who have the time to soak in the Himalaya.

Who can do this: Everyone, age and fitness levels no bar.

How long: 8 days.

When: Summer and monsoon (if you are okay with crossing landslides).

- Day 1: Reach Chandigarh and drive to Shimla or a little ahead to Fagu.
- Day 2: Long drive to reach Sangla. Can stay in one of the nice camps by the river.
- Days 3–5: Spend time in Sangla, similar to what we did. Walk to the Rakcham Glacier, visit Kamru Fort and definitely visit Chitkul. Walk to Nagasthi if up for it.
- Day 6: Drive to and stay in Kalpa. Just the view of Kinner Kailash is worth this diversion from the main route.
- Day 7: Return journey. Visit Sarahan on the way towards Shimla. Stay at Narkanda or Fagu.
- Day 8: Drive back to Chandigarh for flight / train back.

ITINERARY 16:
THE KINNER KAILASH TREK

Category: Trek.

Recommended for: Trekkers who are looking for the next challenge.

Who can do this: Experienced trekkers with good fitness levels.

How long: 10 days.

When: July to September.

- Day 1: Reach Chandigarh and drive to Shimla or a little ahead to Fagu.
- Day 2: Long drive to reach Kalpa.
- Day 3: Rest and acclimatise in Kalpa. Explore the market and the monasteries.
- Days 4–7: Trek starts from Lambar and passes Charang village, before crossing the Charang Ghati Pass into Chitkul.
- Day 7: Trek ends in Chitkul. Can stay there or just ahead in Sangla.
- Day 8: If you have time in hand, spend a day relaxing in Sangla.
- Day 9: Return journey. Visit Sarahan on the way towards Shimla. Stay at Narkanda or Fagu.
- Day 10: Drive back to Chandigarh for flight / train back.

ITINERARY 17: TREKS INTO SANGLA (THERE ARE MANY, JUST MENTIONING TWO)

Category: Trek.

Recommended for: Off-beat trek lovers.

Who can do this: Prior trek experience and good fitness levels.

How long: 9 to 10 days.

When: May to October.

ITINERARY 17A: PABBAR VALLEY TO SANGLA OVER BURAN GHATI PASS

- Day 1: Reach Chandigarh and drive to Shimla or a little ahead to Fagu.
- Day 2: Drive and reach Janglik in Pabbar Valley. This is the trek start point.
- Days 3–7: A five-day trek across Buran Ghati Pass takes you to Sangla Valley.
- Day 7–9: Similar to last three days in Itinerary 16.

ITINERARY 17B:
HARSIL TO SANGLA OVER LAMKHAGA PASS

Category: Tough trek.

- Day 1: Reach Uttarkashi from Dehradun.
- Day 2: Drive and reach the beautiful village of Harsil.
- Days 3–8: A six-day trek brings you to Sangla over the Lamkhaga Pass. Very remote and a lot of glacier crossings.
- Days 8–10: Similar to Itinerary 16.

LOCAL CONTACTS

1. Chander Mohan Negi from Kalpa helped us organise the Kinner Kailash trek. Contact 9805530056.
2. Banjara Camps and Kinner Camps are the two best places to stay in Sangla.
3. Pankaj Negi from Janglik can help you organise the Buran Ghati trek. Contact 9805227768.

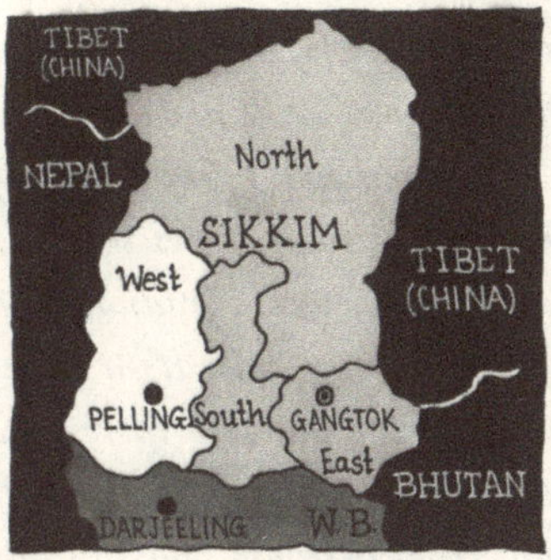

Hand-drawn maps for representation purposes only.
Not to scale.

SIKKIM

A long night in Thangu

Sikkim is conveniently divided into east, west, north and south districts. Kangchendzonga, the third-highest mountain in the world, dominates the landscape and is visible from pretty much all corners of the small state. While the majority Nepali population of Sikkim lives in the east, west and the southern parts, the original inhabitants, the Lepchas, and the first migrants, the Bhotiyas, are concentrated in the north. Both these groups practice Tibetan Buddhism to varying degrees.

For a small state, the terrain varies dramatically, from the foothills at about 600 metres, to the northern plateau at 4,000 metres, to the Kangchendzonga top at 8,500+ metres. The diversity of the Himalayan ranges, which are 400-kilometre wide at most places, is condensed in less than 200 km here. From Gangtok, as we move towards the north, the road passes through thick jungles, characteristic of Sikkim, while gradually gaining height. I call it a road, it's anything but. It's a bone-crushing ride, to put it mildly. During our trip there in 2012, everyone held on for dear life as only the skill of the local drivers got us through. The 120 km took us more than eight hours. (Note—the road is much better now.) The saving graces were the utterly amazing forests and mountains throughout the drive.

From Mangan, the road splits into two—towards Lachen and Lachung. From time immemorial, these two villages have been the gateway to the wonders of north Sikkim—the trans-Himalayan plateau and high altitude lakes (Gurudongmar at 4,800 metres is the most popular) similar to Ladakh, but with more vegetation due to the different latitude.

We spent a couple of easy days in Lachen, acclimatising for the journey ahead and also learning a bit about the local people and their way of life during our short walks in the village, while relishing their food, pickles and home-made brews.

Most tourists follow a standard itinerary to north Sikkim. After spending a night in Lachen, they leave early morning for the long drive to Gurudongmar Lake and come back exhausted by evening. In the rush of the day, the small village of Thangu is usually missed out or a quick stop for lunch is made there. Rarely, if ever, is the monastery above the village visited. It is the same with the beautiful Chopta Valley, just ahead of Thangu and only ten minutes off the main road. Our plan was to spend a night in Thangu, see the monastery, explore the Chopta Valley and go to Gurudongmar the next day. This story is of the long night in Thangu.

Two days of chilling around in the relative luxury of the guesthouse in Lachen, under the guise of acclimatisation of course, set the stage for what was to come over the next two days. Set the contrast, I should say.

'We love this place, how will it be in Thangu?' Shweta asked on everyone's behalf. I tried my best to paint a realistic picture, considering that I had never been to Thangu myself. There is hardly any material about the village in books or online. My description was based on my previous experience of homestays in remote villages of the Himalaya.

'Villages like Thangu are usually very quiet. People are either working hard in the fields or at home and are very shy about talking to city people like us. So take the initiative and engage them in conversation. The homestays are neat and clean. The host takes extra effort to ensure we are comfortable. But be considerate when asking for anything. It's not a guesthouse or a hotel. As long as you keep an open mind, you will love the experience,' was my long answer to a short question.

We left Lachen and continued further north along the Teesta River. The thick forest, the kind you will only see in Sikkim Himalaya, continued to be our companion. The road was worse, if that was possible, than the one leading up to Lachen. All of us were far more relaxed though, silently admiring the human ability to adapt and familiarise ourselves to our surroundings. I have seen that happen on all my trips, how everyone reacts to the same situation so differently once they have had a small exposure to it.

Just after Lachen, we crossed the Teesta River, and with that, entered the realm of the trans-Himalaya. (Lachen means 'the big pass' as it literally allows you to pass across the Greater Himalayan range, and has been historically a crucial trade route to Tibet.)

We were deep in the Himalaya now, and it was hard to believe that, just 150 km ago, we were in the foothills. But that's what Sikkim offers—all the diversity of the Himalaya packaged neatly and compactly.

'How long will this forest continue, I want to see something else,' said a mildly-impatient Sneha, and before I could give her my well-practised speech, the valley started opening up. The mountains appeared to be much taller and grander, the vegetation changed and the thick forest was replaced by pastures … and just like that, we were in a different world. A world which seemed like it was just waiting for us, tucked away around the bend on the road. Take a look at the picture on page xv of the inserts.

A packed village with no one around

The drivers were excited too, not by the sights like we were, but because this meant Thangu was close. The signs were there. Buddhist prayer flags on tall wooden poles, cultivated fields and small storage spaces for food grains—typical markers on the outskirts of a Himalayan village. But it was the villagers who were conspicuous by their absence. Not a person was in sight, on the road, or in the fields or just chilling by the wayside as the Himalayan people always do. The drivers too were wondering what was up, as they didn't get to meet and greet the acquaintances they seem to have in every village. Soon enough, the village of Thangu was in sight, but like it happens all the time in the mountains, it took us a long time to get there.

We finally crossed a small bridge and reached the village, only to be greeted by an eerie scene: lots and lots of vehicles lined up on the only road—buses, tempos, jeeps, SUVs, small cars, etc.—but no one around. Total silence. The village had about twenty homes on both sides of the road and all of them were locked. Most of the homes had a small shop / eating place on the ground floor and some rooms on the first floor. A few had 'homestay available' boards also. I had never spoken to our homestay host directly as there was no reliable network here, but had booked it through a friend in Sikkim, and the host had confirmed just a few days back. After looking around for a few minutes, I managed to find our homestay. It was also locked from outside.

'You didn't mean this kind of quiet, right?' Charlton

asked me rhetorically. The silence was inexplicable. Our drivers tried to make calls but there was no network. We spread out in the small market trying to look for someone. Thankfully, the mystery was resolved soon enough when a kind stranger, who was startled to see us, like we were on seeing him, told us what was happening. We had reached Thangu on the biggest day of its social calendar.

It was the annual festival at the monastery in Thangu, one of the biggest in north Sikkim. People from all over north Sikkim had gathered there today, along with the villagers. The highlight of the festival is the masked dance performed at the monastery courtyard. And it was starting just about now, we were told.

'Let's go, we will sort out the homestay later,' I said, and everyone was more than willing. The monastery was perched on the other side of a nearby hill. We drove till the makeshift parking lot (more vehicles) and then walked up. We could hear the traditional Tibetan trumpets just as we neared the top, and with our hearts thumping with the exertion and excitement, we put in one final effort and reached the monastery.

And the first thing that we saw was, people. Hundreds of them. Wearing their best clothes and jewellery, sitting in the courtyard in a circle, with a large empty space in the middle. The monastery was to our left, with its door closed. On one side was a group of monks playing traditional festival music. The buzz in the air was palpable. The beat suddenly changed, the door opened and out came the first batch of the masked dancers.

Guests of honour in a masked dance

If you have not seen one live, it's very difficult to explain how a masked dance flows. Do check the picture on page xvi of the inserts to get an idea. It usually starts with a slow rhythmic beat and the dancers go clockwise, taking two steps forward and one back. Then, sometimes, two main actors step in the middle and enact a scene, usually a battle, not necessarily between good and evil, but just between two different characters. As they fight, the music picks up speed and the movements become faster and faster, ultimately reaching a crescendo as the dance / scene comes to an end and the dancers march back inside. After some time, the next group comes and performs their version. There were groups from different places in the entire district and we were thrilled to witness this, especially because it was not part of the itinerary.

Not just that, we had inadvertently become the guests of honour. I had attended masked dance ceremonies in big monasteries in Ladakh and even in Spiti. Usually, there are always many tourists, especially foreigners, with their big cameras. You are just one of the many spectators. Here, on the other hand, because it was so remote and not a 'popular' monastery, we were the only non-Sikkimese, and by default, the red carpet was rolled out for us. We were escorted to the front of the crowd and some seats were cleared for us. In between the performances, we were asked if we wanted to go backstage and meet the performers, which we did, clicking pictures with the dancers, seeing them get ready and even handling the masks. To top it all, after the dances were over, we were taken to the 'VIP' lunch, and were the first ones to eat.

'Just smile and eat before they get any wiser,' instructed Charlton and we did exactly that. Then we said our byes and slowly walked back. As soon as we turned the bend, we burst out into laughter and high-fived each other. It was full paisa vasool, and we hadn't even paid for it.

Our euphoria remained even when we figured out that all the villagers, including our homestay host, were still in the monastery and would perhaps be there for a couple of more hours. And when I suggested a quick visit to the nearby Chopta Valley, a beautiful, wide, mystical place, the idea was greeted with much enthusiasm. We got back into the cars and drove for fifteen more minutes, and took a left turn to once again enter a new world. Pardon my use of 'new world' so often, but I am restricted by limited vocabulary to describe the scale and beauty of Himalaya. Do check the picture on page xvi of the inserts. The valley was at its widest just before meeting the Teesta, a wide river bed with some parts under cultivation and some cottages being constructed by the Sikkim tourism department. As we walked deeper into the valley it became narrower, more mysterious, and the possibility of thrill and adventure further along was irresistible. In fact, there is a beautiful trail further ahead which is used by shepherds, and which, from April to June, overflows with flowers including the rhododendron. We all looked longingly towards the valley, took some pictures and walked back to the car. Perhaps someday we would trek here, but right now, it was time to check-in.

Trouble in paradise

Thangu was a changed place when we returned. It was swarming with people in high spirits and also high on spirits. Really. Every 'hotel' on the ground floor of each home was packed and chang and arak were flowing freely. Men, women, everyone was partaking. Our drivers told us that, today, it's almost officially sanctioned to drink as much as you can and then dance for as long as you can. Some visitors from other villages would leave in the evening while many would stay back and the merriment would go on.

I tracked down our homestay host, who was running around serving drinks and momos to his 'guests'. When I reminded him of our stay at his place that night, he first looked at me in amazement, then offered me a drink and with a sheepish smile told me, 'Sorry, sir, but important Lamas have come and I had to offer my rooms to them.' He quickly added, 'But don't worry, sir. I am sure you will find rooms somewhere in the village.'

I took a sip of the chang he was offering me to steady my nerves, came out and came clean—'We have to find another place to stay, Lamas have taken our rooms.' I recruited the drivers along with rest of the group and we started the door-to-door campaign of finding shelter for the night. Every house in the village was packed that night with 'important Lamas' or 'friends from so and so village'. Finally, just when we were about to give up, one guy agreed to give us some rooms. When I went in, I figured that 'some rooms' meant exactly two, one upstairs and a very small room on the ground floor. And the only reason they were available was because they were possibly the dirtiest in the village. There was a small conference between our group and the drivers to discuss our strategy. It went something like this:

Us: How cold will it get in the night?
Drivers: Below freezing.
Us: So we can't sleep outdoors?
Drivers: No.
Us: So we have to sleep in these rooms?
Drivers: Yes.

When there are not many options, you will be surprised how quickly decisions are made.

'C'mon guys, it will be a unique experience. These people are celebrating their biggest day of the year. They are going to party all night, and if nothing else, we will be entertained. We are in fact lucky to be here today and this is a very small price to pay,' I played the team leader. Somehow it worked. All pumped, we started with the mission 'night in Thangu'. It was decided that the rooms needed to be cleaned first, then beddings gathered and arranged in a way that we could all fit into the two rooms. We finally had to ensure that everyone had enough blankets.

'Mission clean up' took about thirty minutes and we managed to transform the big room upstairs from a dump of bidi stubs to a semi-acceptable dorm room. The small room downstairs was not that bad to begin with. Small mercies.

Charlton, Prashant and Venu, the gang from Australia,

staked their claim to the smaller room on the ground floor. It was just an annexe to the storeroom and had two single beds plus some space on the floor to put a bedding or two.

'It is perfect for us,' Venu declared. The rest of the group occupied the room above by default. With this settled, it was time for some tea. Just next door was a small shop cum restaurant run by a Nepalese woman, Sai, and her cousins who were visiting her from Gangtok. That became our adda. We occupied it at around 5 p.m. and didn't leave till it was 7 p.m. Most of the time was spent watching with amusement the way Sai handled drunken men (and women) who stumbled into the shop to order food. She pushed out or shouted at most for being useless, asked some to sit quietly and eat, and flirted with the good-looking ones. She was strong and decisive, and everyone loved her for that. It helped that we were treated consistently well, and that our tea and momos were served with a smile. After all, we were the only sober people in Thangu that night.

Around 7 p.m., our new homestay host came to the shop and requested us to have dinner before his hotel got packed for the night. We said our byes to Sai and her cousins, and stepped inside our homestay. It was dark and it took some time for our eyes to adjust. There were people sitting around with glasses of chang / arak / beer in their hands. In the middle of the living room was a big bukhari, the traditional wood-fed heater of the high Himalayan homes, keeping the place warm. Some men and women were tending to it constantly. On one side was the open kitchen and a table was laid out with our food. We picked up our plates, served ourselves and sat at the prime seats vacated for us. The food was very good, but we were more interested in the locals who had started playing a musical instrument and singing songs. It was fun and we were getting into the groove too, looking forward to a nice evening of song and dance and being part of the festivities. Little did we know that the singing and dancing would continue all night long, would almost burn the house down and give Charlton a panic attack.

Fire on the mountain–run, run, run

Let's use our imagination a bit now, to get a bird's eye view of the happenings in the homestay that night—we are looking down at a dark room from the top. When our eyes focus, we can see that the room is full of people, men and women, who all look like they belong here, singing, talking, laughing, drinking something from dirty mugs. There are also a few others, men and women, who are clearly looking out of place, with their clothes, with their stares and with the plates of food in their hands. Some of those who belong are getting up now and forming a circle in the middle of the room, just beside the bukhari. They begin moving in a slow, rhythmic manner, taking their cue from the bards who are singing loudly now. After each song, there is a lot of cheering and laughter and a few more get into the circle.

When the visitors are done with their food, their leader is pulled into the circle, and he in turn pulls in a couple of his group members. The outsiders become insiders and everyone is excited. The singing is more purposeful and a couple of steps are added to the rhythmic dance. The visitors are trying valiantly to match the grace of the locals, but don't seem to have much control over their limbs, flailing them wildly. But it's all fun, everyone is laughing, especially the three middle-aged men from the visitor's group.

Songs blend into each other, time passes and some of the visitors are looking fidgety. They look at each other, and when the first one moves out of the circle, she is quickly followed by two more. They are standing outside now, clapping and still smiling, but it appears as if they are wondering when this will end. But the locals appear to be just warming up. Every now and then, one of them will jump into the middle of the circle and either sing loudly or dance madly, clearly effected by whatever they have been drinking. The visitors can't understand the songs but they are becoming raunchy, like all folk songs do, and there is plenty of flirting happening. It now appears that the visitors have served their purpose and the dancing is well and truly taken over by the locals. They are saying their byes, but they are not sure if anyone is paying attention. They quickly move out and go upstairs to their room, but within five minutes, the three men come back and join the dance again. They are now dancing more freely, perhaps uninhibited in the absence of their friends.

It's 10 p.m. and it appears that the three are getting tired. It's tough to keep up with locals in any case. Stepping out of the circle, they say their reluctant byes and head to their small room adjoining the hall. Through the door we can see them crashing in their beds. Goodnight to them. Wait, maybe not so fast, as the leader of the group has just come down from the first floor with his bedding and blanket. He heads straight into the small room, talks to them for a minute, rolls his bed out on whatever little space is left on the floor and lies down. Outside, the dancing, singing, cheering, drinking is going just one way—higher. It is way too loud to sleep and the four can be seen moving around restlessly in their beds, talking (one can assume) about when this will end. Enough already, as they say in their world. One of them comes out and asks everyone to keep it a little quiet. They try to pull him back into the dancing circle, and he somehow manages to extricate himself and rush back inside the room.

It is well past midnight now and the dancing has degenerated into drunken swaying. One particular person is all over the place, and before he can be restrained, he has bumped into the bukhari and has knocked out some burning logs along with a can of kerosene lying close by. The floor is wooden. Mayhem ensues. Some people run out shrieking, some are trying to diffuse the embers, some are beating up the culprit and some are still swaying. A lot of people from the next door homes have gathered outside and even the drivers of the group are up. They, along with Sai, are amongst the few sober ones and are now taking charge. Luckily, none of the wood splinters caught the kerosene and they are all extinguished in time. In the entire din, no one is able to hear the desperate banging and shouts from inside the room. Let's go there.

Behind a locked door

A quick recap leading up to the locked room—

My original plan was to sleep upstairs with the rest of the group. We were chatting, cracking jokes and when some people fell asleep, the rest of us stood out in the balcony in the cold night, looking up at the stars. We had no clue that the three Australians had dodged us and were dancing downstairs. Instead, I was feeling a bit guilty that they were all by themselves and decided to sleep with them in case they needed any help. The others agreed. I picked up my bedding and blanket, and went downstairs. By that time, they were back in their room, lying on their beds, but not asleep as yet. They seemed glad that I was there, and made space for me on the floor, at the same time complaining mildly about the loud sounds of the singing and dancing outside. I told them to ignore it and try to sleep, as we had an early start the next day.

Half an hour must have passed. I was half asleep when I felt that someone was standing right above me. I opened my eyes and saw a woman, who I soon recognised as the lady of the house. She put a finger on her lips to tell me to be quiet, crawled over me and went inside the adjoining store. After a couple of minutes, while I lay there stunned, she returned with a smile on her face, a carton of beer bottles in hand, and whispered to me, 'So jao.' She then crawled over me and went outside. It was surreal. I didn't or couldn't utter a word.

'Listen to what she said, and sleep,' I told myself. I didn't know at that time, but on her way back, she had locked the door from outside, perhaps out of habit, or maybe because they didn't want us to interrupt them. Who knows?

I had just managed to fall asleep when a loud noise woke me up. Charlton and Prasad were banging on the door and trying to peek outside through the crack.

'What's happening, guys?'

'Can't you smell kerosene? There is gonna be a fire and we are locked inside a wooden room,' Charlton was hyper. Venu was looking at them with a confused expression. I figured that, like me, he had no clue as to what was happening. Later, we would all realise that since Venu and I were sleeping on the floor, we didn't smell the kerosene fumes. The other two, who were on the bed, did. Charlton left the door and attacked the small window, trying to see if he could get out from there. But he couldn't open that either. I peeped outside and realised that there was utter chaos. No one was going to hear us. By now, Charlton was sitting on his bed with his eyes wide open and staring into space.

'Looks like he is having a panic attack,' guessed Venu, to which Charlton replied with another cold stare.

We tried the window again, and this time we managed to open it. That seemed to help and Charlton breathed a little easy. Venu stood glued to the crack in the door and was witness to the arrival of Sai and our drivers, and the quick salvaging of the situation. He was giving us all non-stop commentary about what was happening outside. And all of us listened with the attention of villagers in their sixties listening to cricket commentary.

'And now the splinters have been doused … the kerosene has been removed from the scene … the drunkards have been kicked out … the party is over guys.' But what about us? Our friends had apparently slept through this whole ruckus and no one remembered that we were in the room. Finally, when everything was settled, the lady remembered. Still on a high, she opened the door and with a smile said, 'Ab so jao.' And so, just like that, the adventure finally ended, with the four of us lying down in a small room with the window and door wide open, the cool breeze blowing the kerosene fumes away and the stars smiling down on us.

P.S.: The next morning, we were greeted by a red-eyed but surprisingly bubbly Charlton. 'I couldn't sleep all night, but what an experience, wow, I will never forget it,' he said. He, and all of us, were to add another to the 'never forget list' when we drove north-wards, entered a new world, surprise, surprise, this time with a terrain similar to that of Ladakh. We saw Indian Army tanks right under huge snow-covered mountains and finally reached the Gurudongmar Lake at a height of 4,800 metres. Amongst the highest fresh water lakes in the world, it is fed by a huge glacier which comes all the way to the banks of the lake. With its atmosphere of serenity, the calm and gentle sound of small waves, Gurudongmar Lake offers an experience far too ethereal to be described by accidental writers like me. I have put up a picture on page xvi of the inserts, that's the best I can do.

P.S. 2: During most of the trips to the Himalaya, strong bonds are formed between complete strangers and everyone keeps in touch through WhatsApp groups and reunions. Paradoxically, the WhatsApp group of this Sikkim trip is called 'Thugs of Thangu'.

THE GUIDE

Oh, there are just so many trips you can plan in Sikkim. The west, east, south and north, all have multiple options. But there are always some places which are less crowded and can still give you all the pros of the more popular ones. In addition, Sikkim is the only other place, apart from Ladakh and Spiti, with an organised network of homestays. Make sure that your trip includes at least a night in a homestay. Here are my top three favourite trips from Sikkim.

ITINERARY 18:
THE SIKKIM INITIATION

Category: Road trip with short walks.

Recommended for: Those who want to see Sikkim at its best.

Who can do this: Everyone, age and fitness levels no bar.

How long: 7 days.

When: March to April ideally, also September to November.

- Day 1: Fly into Bagdogra or take the train to NJP. Drive to Darjeeling.
- Day 2: Drive to Sombaria, on the outskirts of the sanctuary in west Sikkim. Stay the night in a guesthouse.
- Day 3: A day walk in the Barsey Rhododendron Sanctuary to see the blooming flowers. Back to Sombaria.
- Day 4: Drive to central Sikkim and stay at a homestay in Kewzing village.
- Day 5: Explore the 17th-century Tashiding monastery, one of the prettiest in Sikkim.
- Day 6: Drive to Gangtok in east Sikkim. Spend the day chilling. Alternatively, instead of Gangtok, stay in nearby Rumtek.

- Day 7: Drive back to Bagdogra / NJP.

  Note: Can extend the stay by a day in Darjeeling and / or Gangtok. Can also split this itinerary into two shorter trips.

ITINERARY 19: THE NORTH SIKKIM ADVENTURE

Category: Road trip plus short walks.

Recommended for: Those okay with long drives and high places.

Who can do this: Everyone, basic fitness levels.

How long: 7 to 9 days.

When: April or September to October.

- Day 1: Fly into Bagdogra or take the train to NJP. Drive to Rumtek near Gangtok and stay for the night.
- Day 2: Drive to and stay in Lachen.
- Day 3: Extra day here is worth it to rest and acclimatise.
- Day 4: Drive to and stay in Thangu. Visit the monastery and Chopta Valley.
- Day 5: Drive to and visit Gurudongmar Lake. Return to Lachen.

- Day 6: Drive to and stay in Gangtok for the night.
- Day 7: Drive back to Bagdogra / NJP.

Options: You can add two days for Lachung and a visit to Yumthang Valley (called the Valley of Flowers of the east).

ITINERARY 20: THOLUNG MONASTERY—THE LAND OF LEPCHAS

Category: Road trip plus a trek.

Recommended for: Those interested in history and totally off-beat places.

Who can do this: Everyone, basic fitness levels.

How long: 8 days.

When: April or September to October.

- Day 1: Fly into Bagdogra or take the train to NJP. Drive to Kalimpong.
- Day 2: Drive to Mangan and stay in a homestay. Mangan is the gateway to north Sikkim and also to Dzongu, the land of Lepchas.
- Day 3: Drive into Dzongu and stay in the village of Tingvong in a homestay.
- Day 4: Drive to the trek starting point for the Tholung monastery. Trek to Tholung and stay the night in one of the trekker huts.

- Day 5: A day in Tholung. Visit the historic monastery, also go for a walk in the forest ahead.
- Day 6: Back to the road and drive to Mangan.
- Day 7: Drive to Gangtok. You will have the whole day in Gangtok.
- Day 8: Drive back to Bagdogra / NJP.

IN THE FOOTSTEPS OF THE YETI

Instead of going north from Mangan, if you go west, you will reach Dzongu, a land reserved for the Lepchas of Sikkim, the original inhabitants. They traditionally follow a unique blend of Buddhism and nature worship. At the head of the valley is the historic and remote Tholung monastery. Amongst the most sacred monasteries in Sikkim, it has, stored away, some of the most precious Buddhist artefacts and relics, kept here for safekeeping, so remote is this place. These are taken out once every three years for display. Beyond Tholung, it's wild land. Only yak herders go to the pastures around Kishong Lake.

For them, the Yeti or Migoo as it's called here, is as real as you and me. It whistles from the high mountains (beyond which lies Kangchendzonga) as it eyes the yaks for lunch. One of the passes is called Migoo La, the Pass of the Yeti. Latest research points to the possibility of a type of bear that has adapted to the high Himalaya. Whatever the case, you can trek to Kishong Lake and find out for yourself.

LOCAL CONTACTS

1. To plan all aspects of your trip to Sikkim, HELP Tourism is a good option. http:/www.helptourism.com
2. Homestays in west and central Sikkim are organised and booked by Kangchendzonga Conservation Committee (KCC) at kcc_sikkim@hotmail.com and Kewzing Tourism Development Committee (KTDC) at ktdc@sikkimfoundation.org.

MY SOLO MISADVENTURE

Rujuta Diwekar

Never before in my life had i felt something like this.

'No, i will go alone,' i said to Stefan. 'Will you stay back and wait for me?' i asked earnestly. He didn't need to and he probably shouldn't, i thought. He was in India for a short time and spending two nights in Netala after the yoga course was over, just waiting for me to return from my solo trek, was clearly asking for too much.

'Yes, i will,' he said, almost emotionlessly, a state that i had begun to understand as his normal state of being. Ah, kambakht ishq happens to everyone and it was in full bloom in my heart at this point. It was May 2005 and i had just completed a full month course at the Sivananda Yoga Vedanta Academy at Netala, Uttarkashi. My teacher, Swami Govindanandaji's teachings had a profound effect on me and i was convinced that fear, like happiness, was just a state of mind. Just a year ago, my trek mate and i had experienced a 'ghost' while camping near Gaumukh. The dread we had felt, lasted for at least three to four hours that night. We called it a ghost because we couldn't see anyone and then, post the course, Swamiji had said that it was just my mind, not anything outside. And even if there was anything outside, it was a creation of my mind, a creation of fear. It was me superimposing what was inside on the outside, telling myself to break away from the bond of people and perceptions. It's because i didn't know my mind, and if you know that you don't know, then you are in a good place. That's the gist of what i learnt in a month.

But this is about the trek. So, to overcome my fears and more importantly my mind, post the thirty days in the ashram, i decided to go on my first solo trek ever. With a guide, a cook and a porter, i mean. It was a time of no cell phones, well, almost no cell phones, and i didn't have to report to anyone back home about my plans. i was like every other person of my age then, mid-twenties and in a clueless relationship with myself and others. To begin with, i marched to Uttarkashi and went to the first trekking office that i saw. The only credibility they had was that they were right across the bus depot, but then in the Himalaya, you trust everyone—that i had learnt from my very first trek in 1995.

'No, we won't go with you.'

'Why?' i demanded.

'You are a single girl that's why.'

'Arre dar mere ko lagna chahiye na? i won't be a problem for you. Sab responsibility mera, okay? Tell me a trek that is beautiful and surreal, max two nights.'

He fell for my Bambaiya speech and confidence, and just like that, my trek to Dayara Bugyal was fixed.

A Tata Sumo came with the trekking goods to pick me up from the Netala ashram the next day. It was a short drive of 8 km to Netala, but a different world from the buzzing and the broken town (earthquakes and landslides) of Uttarkashi. The ashram, which until the day before, had twenty-five people from many different countries, was now empty. Nothing. Just the sound of the Bhagirathi, the bells of the temple and the winds from the forest above. Swamiji was resting, a much-needed rest after having to deal with so many of us for over a month. Stefan was not there too; he was walking somewhere in the mountains across the river, but without his backpack. So he planned to be back in the ashram by evening.

In that moment, my heart sank just a little bit at the prospect of never being able to say bye to Stefan, never being able to see him again, but my fears were more important than my sheeshe wala dil, so off i went.

We drove up towards Gangotri, with the Bhagirathi in full flow to our right. To me, the drive from Uttarkashi to Gangotri, the full 100 km, is the best ever. There's always the river by your side, there's India's most beautiful valley, Harsil, and there's the fact that you can actually make it in just three hours flat. Oh, the joy of good roads. But today, we cut towards the left much before Harsil, much before the tall trees disappeared and the rocky mountains appeared. We were headed to Barnala, the roadhead before Dayara Bugyal.

Barnala is your typical picturesque Himalayan village—cute kids, beautiful women, robust men, furry dogs, views … you name it. And from here, the trekking party started. All of us were excited. The team had never trekked with just a girl, and i had never trekked alone. We climbed up the shaded, easy gradient path and crossed many shepherd shelters that were almost camouflaged in the mountains. They were impressed with my walking, and me with their talking. Easy banter, local trivia, folk songs and we moved on. And in no time at all, we came across a huge opening in the forest with a small pond at its centre. Barnala Taal—trees in the backdrop, with tiny flowers spread all over the meadow and snow peaks reflecting in its still waters. When you come to a patch like this, you know that you have come home. To the home of the mighty Gujjars, who come up to the meadows with their families, kids and dogs along with the 'walking and grazing on the freshest grass' cattle in summer. They then move the whole entourage down for the winter.

If words could express it, i would describe what i felt. But what words can possibly describe how stable the mind feels after a long walk in the woods? How deeply it enjoys the beauty of every tiny thing, how sensitively the senses perceive and how joyful the heart feels? It's one of those 'do it to know it' kinda things. So we proceeded to a 'chattri' a little above the pond. Chattri is like a little structure with a tin roof, with a concrete ground and a concrete bench to sit on. It's like one of the things we see around sunset points. But on a trek, this is invaluable. It blocks the wind from three sides, gives you a flat ground for the kerosene stove and a roof that protects you from sun and the rain. All four of us sat down and had our first round of lemon tea with biscuits, a trekking tradition. A stimulant before the real job of cooking and pitching tents. Two shepherd dogs got a whiff of the foreign scent and made their way to check us out. The Barnala Taal was their area, and they were the official utsav murti. They would decide if we could stay for the darshan of the divine or whether we must be barked away.

'What is this?' i asked the cook, pointing at the thick barbed wire around their necks.

'Protection,' he replied.

'From whom?'

'Bagh se.'

'You have tigers here?'

'No, leopards,' said the guide.

Leopard attacks on the cattle are a frequent occurrence and when the dogs stick their necks out to protect them, it's important that the leopard doesn't take them away instead. The barbed wire ensures just that. Soon we were joined by a young boy wearing jeans and t-shirt, from the Gujjar family. One more round of chai. Some more news on life in Uttarkashi and the weather in Barnala Taal. The customary gaalis to the Forest Department were given; the government wants the Gujjars to settle down. They think that the forest belongs to the government and that the cattle spoil the grass. Rubbish. No one lives more in tune with nature than the Gujjars, Bakarwals and the Gaddis. If you settle the walking, nomadic folks in the dusty towns of Haridwar or the like, you not just take away their way of life, you bring upon them diseases and issues of integration; you remove them from life itself.

My team proceeded to make dal chawal and papad, and i decided to stare at the gorgeous Barnala Taal till the end of time. Time doesn't move, but the mind does. The end of time ended in some thirty minutes and we were a happy bunch enjoying our early lunch. There was nothing to do, no distraction of my Mumbai life, ashram, Stefan, nothing. i was in a zone where nothing other than that moment mattered. Rarely in life does one feel that they'd rather be nowhere else but here, with just themselves, without the desire for company or amusement. i was just there. And in that state, post lunch, i decided to move away from the chattri, find a spot, open my yoga mat and well, meditate. Or more like what Swami Govindananda had said—post lunch, spend some time in Vajrasana and that 'rumm' was the root sound of the Manipura (digestion) chakra—so say some mantra with that root. It's amazing how you remember things timely when the mind is still. You are at once experimental, non-judgemental and accepting of the outcomes of your actions. Never before or after that day, have i done what i did in that moment—the mantra jaap of 'Ram'—Shri Ram, Ram, Rameti, Rame, Mano Rame … i went twenty-one times in my head.

And like a miracle, Ram appeared. Wearing a chequered lungi, green kurta, a turban on his head, a stick in his hand and a foot wrapped around the stick, he limped towards me. What avatar was this? i wondered? Oh! Ram was a Musalman! The head of the family of Gujjars was standing right in front of me, and for a moment, i had a look of bewilderment in my eyes. He limped further towards me.

'Combiflam hai?' he asked and stretched his hand out.

'Oops,' i said, while getting up. 'Nahi hai boss, nahi hai.'

'Camp pe hai?' he enquired.

'Not sure, may be the guide has it.'

'Lekin aap ke paas nahi hai?'

'Nahi.'

'Koi bhi medicine nahi hai?'

'No, none. Why? What's wrong with you?' i asked.

'Oh, nothing, just back pain.'

If you are an avid trekker or simply a reader of GP's books, you will know that pills are just a thrill for the Himalayan folk. Just half a dose of any painkiller gives them a big high. And to think that city folks have developed so much resistance to these pills, that even four of them a day can't numb the pain. But that's the purity and naivety of these people, something we cannot even wrap our heads around.

He decided not to pursue the medicine conversation any further.

'Where would you like to go first, your place or mine?'

'Yours,' i said, because the whole family hadn't made their appearance yet at the Barnala Taal and i had only met his young boy and the dogs. So he limped ahead and i walked behind him, to his home. The abode included buffalos, goats and sheep, along with some men younger than him, their wives and kids. They lived in makeshift tents on the meadows beyond the Barnala Taal, in the direction of Dayara Bugyal, that's where we would go tomorrow. The customary meet and greet, followed by the usual conversation—how long they would stay here, where would they go from here (even higher), how they cooked, procured ration and sold the milk, etc. Some more gaalis to 'forester' (Forest Department officer), who would demand one litre of ghee every fifteen days and milk every now and then from them.

Then the talk turned to the costumes and jewellery that the women wear, the traditional chandi with stars or trinkets on their caps, like Zeba Bakhtiyar in the movie *Heena*. And then it was my turn to play the host, so we walked back to my camp. The women decided to stay back and only my Ram, his two brothers and all their children followed. Some more chai and i was not required anymore, as the guide, cook and porter had too much news to exchange and some radio commentary to listen to with these men.

Before we knew it, it was time for dinner and time to pitch my tent. It was early evening still.

'Where will you camp?' i asked my team.

'Right here, in the chattri, and we will pitch your tent right next to ours.'

'No, no, no. i haven't come this far to sleep right next to you, i am here to be alone. My tent should be at least 100 metres away from yours.'

Now it was their turn to look at me with both bewilderment and amusement. Anyway, they decided that i should have it my way. We walked for about 100 metres, or more like a hundred steps away from the chattri, and the tent was pitched. It faced away from them but you could almost draw a straight line from my tent to the chattri. We went back to the chattri and had the traditional trek dinner—soup, khichdi, roasted papad with kaccha onion and tamatar.

There is little to do after dinner on a trek.

'So i will go sleep now,' i declared as i got up.

'Sit with us for a while, talk to us,' the team urged.

'No, i will sleep,' i said. i had to change and it was getting very cold.

Once inside the tent, i changed into double layer ka track pants, wore two t-shirts and all the woollens i had bought from the Bhotiya women in Harsil during my last trip—handmade socks, gloves, monkey cap. They had costed only forty-odd bucks each, but they made me feel so snug. i pulled out my torch and opened up the sleeping bag to figure the best sleeping position, the one where i would feel the least effect of the slope. My head would face the entrance of the tent and my feet would be towards the chattri. i went out of the tent to do susu, and then looked up at the sky. The lush green meadows were lit up with flowers shining like stars, the pond glowed with the reflection of the moon, the soft gushing breeze ... Gratitude overwhelmed me. i was so glad for this life, this body, my ability to spend my limited money on a trek and my daring to go out on a trek alone. All this now seemed to be something i had but that which was not mine, like something that is given to you to enjoy and relish, but not to own. i looked upwards again, 'Thank you ya, thank you,' i said. 'That you chose to show me all this, this richness, this wealth of beauty and harmony that i have done nothing to deserve. This day, this night, this moment and how glorious you look right now, i will never forget, never.'

Typically, if i feel anything even 10 per cent like this,

my eyes will go moist and there will be a lump in my throat, but not today. Today was different.

'Good night, Rajesh,' i shouted out to my favourite of the three. He shined his torch on me and I used the spotlight to wave goodnight to the other two. And then i went into my tent. i squatted inside, zipped the first flap and then the second one, all this while holding my gloves in my mouth so that my hands could work. Gloves back on, i crept into my sleeping bag, removed my gloves and zipped the sleeping bag, put the gloves back on, used the shawl as a chaddar and pulled it over the bag. Okay, now? Nothing, wait for sleep. i stared up for a while, but drifted off quickly to sleep. It was complete darkness, silence and solitude. i was impressed even while being asleep that I was sleeping.

i had gone to bed at about 8.30 p.m. and at around 10-ish, according to the glowing hands of my watch, the sheep dogs started barking. The loud echoes of the barking were coming in the way of my sleep and me.

'Withdraw your senses, pull the ears back,' i heard Swami Govindananda's voice in my head and i went back to sleep. At about 11.30 p.m., i woke up again, crawled out of my tent to do susu and repeated the whole process of getting back inside the sleeping bag and falling off to sleep. Sometime later, but i have no clue when, the barking turned to howling, and i opened my eyes from the dream-like state i was in. Dogs cry when they see ghosts, i had heard. Not again, i thought to myself.

'This time i have remembered to count my blessings, to be grateful, so don't pull me out of the tent again,' i pleaded silently to the ghost. But there is no such thing as a ghost, you know that post a month of studying yoga and Vedanta. Just like you sleep to barks, sleep to howls, i told myself. i promptly shut my eyes and tried hard to sleep.

The howling now seemed to come closer to me, as if the dogs were walking towards my tent. Maybe because they see me as a threat to their cattle, i reasoned with myself. You sleep, kuch nahi hoyega. My resolve to not move was pucca, and the dogs were closing in. But sleep was going to win today, fear was going to lose. i continued lying down with eyes closed. And then all of a sudden, the howling stopped and the barking restarted. It was now a competition between barking and howling, loud howling, even louder barking. The dogs seemed to be right outside my tent now, and before i could whip up another pep talk to myself, there was a sound i hadn't heard ever, and it shook every cell of my being. A loud roar, right outside my tent. Till this moment, the only time i had heard roaring was on TV. National Geographic was switched on in Barnala Taal now. Show time!

Oh shit! i turned inside my bag, lying on my stomach, stretched my arm and reached out for the torch. i made desperate attempts to click the torch button but i was wearing gloves and the torch wouldn't turn on. i removed the gloves with my teeth, even while my hands struggled to switch on the torch. The howling, barking and growling was growing all around me. It was like my Olympic moment and just then my torch came on. Still lying on my stomach, i struggled to open the two tent zips just enough to put my torch out, and then i saw it. Two cat eyes staring back at me, not even 10 or 20 metres from my tent.

'Oh shit,' i said aloud and pulled the torch back. i used my hands to cover my head, my torch now lying under my chest, my body blocking all its light.

'No, no, no, put the torch out again,' i shouted to myself. Only the light would scare the bagh. i lifted myself up on my elbows, took the torch, and holding it like a rifle, pointed it back again. Nothing. No cat eyes staring at me, no shadow of dogs behind it, no growling, no barking, no howling. Nothing. I now know what people mean when they say we stared into emptiness. The full canvas was now devoid of colour or sound, everything was blank, and i was shaken. i sat up now and opened the tent flap a little more.

'Oh, shit,' i said again. My pacing heart, my racing thoughts, my shaking hands settled and i decided to do a good turn. i had fought the bagh but my team, what about them? They must be warned. So i put my slippers on, covered my head and mouth with my shawl and walked towards the chattri. Long walk, fast-paced, unsure footing, but i made it.

'Boss,' i called out, 'the leopard is out.'

The three guys were dead to the world and barely moved.

'Boss,' i clapped, no sound, wearing gloves.

'Boss, suno boss, Rajesh.' My guide moved.

'Kya hua, madam?' he had a startled look on his face, like he had seen a ghost.

'No, nothing much, just that the leopard had come (fear), now it's gone (reassurance) but i thought you should know (fact).' Before he could soak it in, i started walking back.

'Madam,' he called out, 'ruk jao, let me drop you to the tent.'

'Arrey, no problem,' i took a step towards the chattri again. 'Mein chali jaungi, don't worry about me. Bas tum ko bolne aayi thi. Woh kya hai ke baagh aaya tha na, toh thoda tum log alert rahena.' And leaving my sleepyheads behind, i was back in my tent. Not even susu this time, straight off to sleep, the adventure had drained me completely.

The birds began to sing before the crack of dawn, announcing that the big boss was about to rise, and lift the veil of darkness that surrounds us all. i woke up, stretched a bit, did my morning ablutions and rolled out my mat for Suryanamaskar out on the meadow. Boy! Was i in a zone or what! What is it about a good night's sleep that it will wash away the fear that gripped you, memories that haunted you and the physical effort that drained you?

A quick six rounds and i felt reborn as a whole new person. And this time, i walked to the chattri with a song on my lips and spring in my feet.

My team was squatting by the stove making tea, not talking. i sat next to them on the concrete bench.

'Kya?' i asked, raising my open palm towards my face, half salaam, half namaste (and actually neither of them), Mumbaiya for 'good morning'.

'Sorry madam,' said one of them.

'What sorry?'

'No, sorry that you couldn't sleep last night.'

'Oh please, i slept like a rock in fact. Bahut achi neend aayi mujhe. Don't i look fresh? i even did Suryanamaskar,' i said, pointing to my still laid out mat. 'What about you guys? Did you sleep well? i hope the leopard didn't come to visit you later,' i joked, very happy with my sense of humour.

He never comes close to the chattri, they informed me. He knows it to be a place of human inhabitation and will avoid it at all cost. They fear us much more than we fear them, after all.

'Aap ke idhar …' they wondered how it could have possibly come to that side.

It was 2005, no one really came on this trek, much less camped at Barnala Taal. Today, i am told, it's a hot spot with trekkers, with over forty tents during season time.

Like Kangana Ranaut says, a whole lot can change in just ten years, and for the Himalaya, it really has. So in all likelihood, the bagh was just on a nightly prowl, going about his usual business, nocturnal that he is. And then the dogs had to give up their usual business of protecting the cattle and make every possible loud call to alert me, loyal that they are once they forge a friendship. And my team? Well, Rajesh spent the entire night sitting outside my tent, a stick and torch in his hand, while i slept away, oblivious to the whole ruckus i had created. My solo adventure had turned into a sarvajanik misadventure for many.

How do you end a story like this? Because this is where it all begins. That your quest to prove something to yourself will always come at the cost of others. Often innocent others, who have nothing to gain from your ride. That nothing, not even a night's sleep, can be achieved alone, it needs support from an entire ecosystem. That we really are meek little meaningless things and the only way to add meaning to our existence is to co-exist. To respect the role every tiny being in the Universe plays in our lives and to live by Her laws. To abide in harmony, honesty and humility, even when the mind wants to do otherwise. So no, there is no end to this story.

But there should be a happy ending to every love story. So post the trek, i drove back to the ashram, hoping to see and say goodbye to you know who. No Stefan to be found, i had to make do with seeing Swamiji, having chai with him and watching him ROFL at my trek story.

'Good, good,' he said. 'Go now or you will miss your bus to Rishikesh from Uttarkashi.'

i started walking back to the jeep and just then my Stefan appeared. Rare is a man who keeps his word, even rarer than a woman who treks alone. Ah! i am filmi and i would have liked to collapse at his sight, like Madhu did at the sight of Arvind Swami in *Roja*. But in real life, you get to walk. So i walked and he walked.

Press the pause button and watch this in slow motion. As we move closer, i go up on my toes, he lifts me just slightly off my feet. How else do you hug a tall German with braided hair that has been left unwashed for a century? Ishq is not just kambakht, it's also pretty unhygienic. There wasn't a word we exchanged, no promises were made, but our eyes yearned to hold this moment in eternity. The hug had to end and it did, for now, there was a bus to catch. And if you are a Mumbai mulgi, you love your practicality more than love itself.

The End.